The BIG Book of Spells & Potions

- **Simple Spells**
- **Voodoo**
- **White Magic**
- **Black Magic**
- **Protection Spells**
- **Healing Spells**
- **Well-Being Spells**
- **Candle Spells**
- **Money Spells**
- **Wicca Spells**

. . . .

Simple Spells

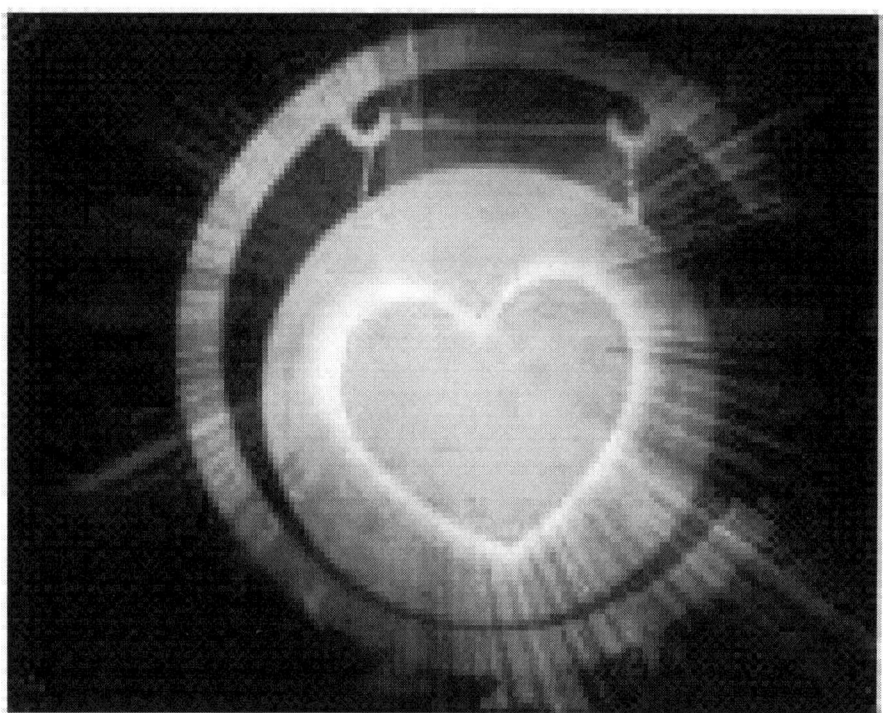

Find That Which Is Lost

A great little spell for misplaced items

Light the candle and put it in a holder that is easy to carry. Begin to walk from room to room with it, repeating the following:

I need what I seek

Please give me a peek

Draw my eyes

To my yearned for prize.

Let your eyes wander around until you are drawn to the place where your item is hiding.

Grow Some Wealth

- A healthy plant

- A coin

- A pinch of dried patchouli

Any plant will do, but if you can get a basil plant, it works better. Just sprinkle a little bit of the patchouli on the soil, then stick the edge of the coin into the soil in the same place so part of the coin is still sticking up out of the dirt.

If some new money materializes in your life, spend that coin right away and put a new one in its place.

A Scattering of Protection

Keep your property safe and sound with a little protection magic.

You will need:

- A handful of salt

- A teaspoon of garlic powder

Mix the salt and garlic together, and sprinkle a pinch of it at each door threshold and windowsill. This will help keep out negative energy.... And vampires. You can't get much easier than this

A Health Blessing

- 1 glass of apple juice

- 1 stick of cinnamon

- 1 white candle

Pour the juice into a glass stirring 4 times with the cinnamon stick. Light the candle and drink a few sips of juice. Repeat the following incantation:

Goddess bless body and soul

Health and wellness is my goal

Finish the rest of the juice and snuff out the candle. Do this spell whenever you feel an illness coming on or even each morning just to stay in tip-top shape. Clear an Argument Spell

For those times when lingering resentment is keeping you from making up with a friend. This can help clear the air and renew your friendship.....

- One bay leaf, dry is fine
- A small paper envelope
- Yellow candle

Write your name on one side of the envelope, and your friend's name on the other. Put the bay leaf inside and seal it. Light the candle and hold the envelope in the flame until it burns. You might want to keep a heat-proof bowl nearby to drop the burning paper into, to save your fingers.

Happiness Candle

- 2 orange candles
- Some dried lavender

Put a few pinches of lavender on your altar or table between the two candles. Light them both and let your hands feel the warmth of the flames. Repeat the following, 7 times:

> This spell please bless
>
> For my happiness

Let the candles burn down and you'll find yourself feeling sunny again in no time. Want another like this? The Wellbeing section has more happiness spells. There is no reason why easy spells have to be dull or meaningless. There are several more pages of these types of spells, so you can keep reading and maybe even add a few of them to your Book of Shadows for that next time you need a quick spell.

End an Argument

For those times when lingering resentment is keeping you from making up with a friend. This can help clear the air and renew your friendship.

- 1 bay leaf
- 1 small envelope
- 1 Yellow candle

Write your name on one side of the envelope, and your friend's name on the other. Put the bay leaf inside and seal it. Light the candle and hold the envelope in the flame until it burns. You might want to keep a heat-proof bowl nearby to drop the burning paper into

Tie Your Troubles In Knots

All you need for this spell is a piece of yarn in the appropriate colour, at least 12 inches long.

Now hold the yarn, with one end in each hand and pull it taut. Think about your problem (just one per spell, please). Concentrate on your difficult situation and start tying knots in the yarn. Visualize all your troubles getting bound up in the knots and trapped there. Keep tying until you feel it's enough.

Take the knotted yarn outside and bury it to keep your problems away.

The Two Halves Of Love

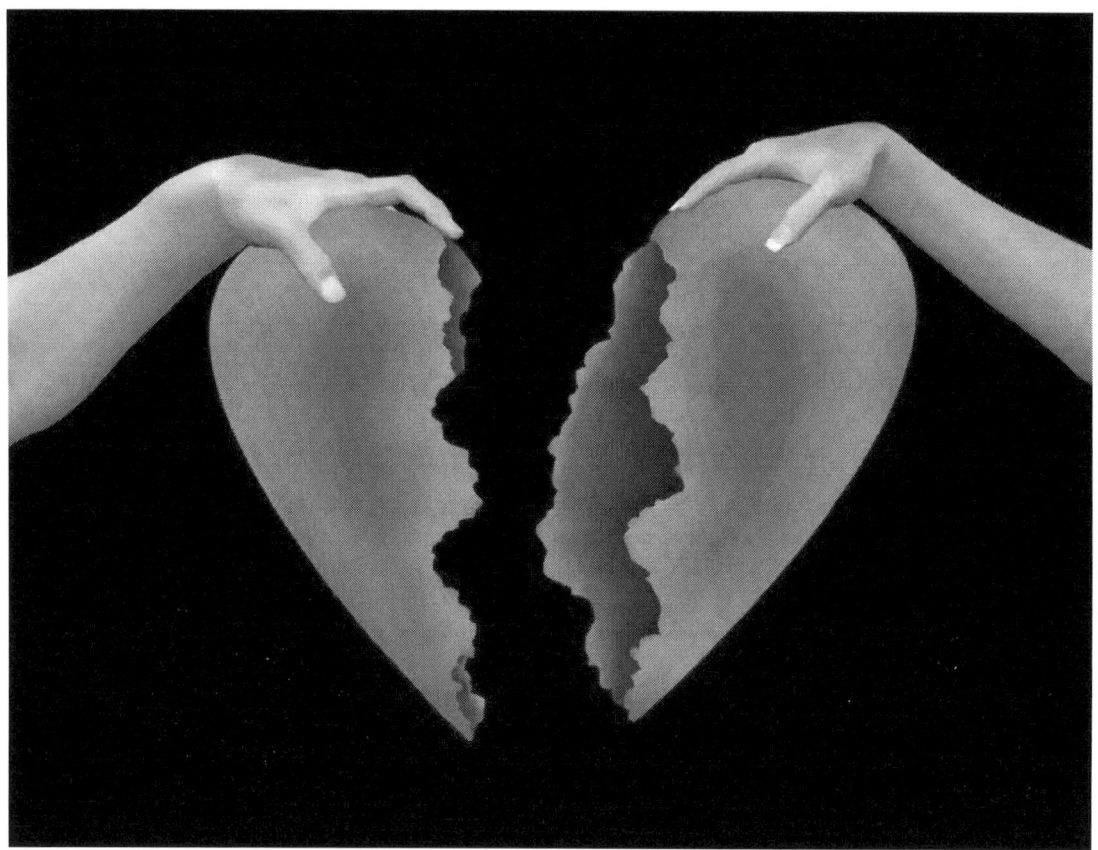

An easy love spell that you can try as you are first learning about witchcraft. You have to get the following supplies:

- 1 Red Candle
- 1 White Candle
- 1 Piece Of Paper
- 1 Pen

Light each candle on your altar, or table where they won't be disturbed. On the paper, write the qualities you are looking for in a partner. Be realistic and keep the list to no more than 6 things.

Tear the paper in half, and burn one half in the red candle flame and the other half over the white candle. An ideal partner should soon come into your life.

Spice Up Your Finances

You don't really need much for supplies, except a dollar bill and some ground cinnamon. You can use any type of paper money, not specifically a dollar... No coins though.

On a Thursday, rub a little cinnamon powder on your finger tip and make 5 separate smudges on your money. Tuck the bill into your purse or wallet where you normally keep money, and leave it there to attract new wealth. That's it.

Be a Love Magnet

- 1 small magnet
- Ylang Ylang oil
- 1 Pink ribbon

Make sure you're using a magnet large enough to tie the ribbon around, so no little button magnets. Rub a little oil into the magnet and then tie ribbon around it with a sturdy knot. Carry it with you to bring some love into your life. Recharge it with more oil on Friday nights until you meet someone new.

Healing Me Candle

Our last easy spell is for healing, and will require you to have 3 light blue candles. Carve your name (or the person you wish the spell to be for) into the wax of all three candles. Set them in holders and light them. Repeat the following:

Healing light,

Shine tonight,

The power I feel,

Be used to heal.

And concentrate on the illness or condition that you are looking to heal. Let the candles burn out on their own when you are done.

Mind Your Step

This is a very easy and simple protection spell to keep harm and negative energy out of your home.

- 3 pieces of broken glass
- 1 rusted nail or screw
- 1 clove of garlic

Dig a hole (at least 6 inches deep) outside your front door, and drop in all the items with the garlic going in last. Cover everything up and stand over the spot. Say out loud:

At this point,

Negativity stops

Then just leave the items in the ground to block out bad influences that might come to your home.

A Peaceful Moment

If you need a little peace in your life, this quick spell will help smooth out a hectic time.

- 1 white feather
- 1 Piece of white thread (several inches long)

Find someplace quiet to do this spell (even in the bathroom if necessary). Tie the feather to the end of the thread. Hold the other end of the thread between your thumb and forefinger, letting the feather dangle in front of your face.

Give it a little puff of air, then watch it swing until hanging still again. As you watch the feather swing, whisper the words:

Still, quiet, hush

I'm not in a rush

Once the feather is still, repeat the lines one more time and your simple spell is done.

Love Struck

Now this one does require that you have a date already, so it may not help you to actually meet someone. If your prospective lover is going to be at your home, give this one a try. In a decorative bowl, mix up the following:

- Half a cup of dried rose petals
- Half a cup of dried lavender
- Pieces of a real vanilla bean
- One tonka bean

You can omit the tonka bean if you can't find a convenient place to get them. Toss in a cinnamon stick instead. Mix it up the day before, and leave the bowl out when he or she is there.

Origami Love

- A pinch of lavender
- A pinch of rosemary
- One piece of orris root
- A piece of stiff red paper

Lay out the paper, and put the herbs in the middle. Fold the paper over a few times to enclose the herbs and make a little "envelope". Seal it shut with a piece of tape or string (don't staple or glue). Carry the little love charm around with you to draw in some romance.

Yarrow Love Charm

It doesn't get much easier than this. I already included this one in with the Wiccan love spells but it certainly qualifies for this page too. All you need is a sprig of yarrow.

You might need to try a florist's shop or herb supplier. It has to be a sprig or branch, NOT chopped or powdered herbs. You have to hang the sprig above your bed (a piece of string or ribbon will do). It has to hang around the middle, bedposts don't count. This is an age-old charm to bring new love.

Melt Away Weight Loss Spell

Few people can say they are happy with their weight, but be honest with yourself about whether you really need to lose those pounds. You can add some simple spell assistance to your weight loss with just a brown candle.

Carve at the top of your candle, your current weight. At the bottom, carve in the weight you'd like to be (realistically). Every night before you go to bed, light the candle for 15 minutes. As the candle wax melts down towards your goal weight, you will start to slim down.

Bury and Banish

If there is someone in your life that you would like to not be involved with anymore, this is the spell for you. All you need is a black sheet of paper. Black construction paper is likely the easiest to find and will work fine.

Write the person's name in the middle, and it doesn't matter if you can't actually read it. It just has to be there. Fold the paper up as small as you can. Take it outside and bury it in the ground. Once it's buried, say the following out loud:

Into the ground

Where you can't be found

You're no longer around

I can't heard your sound

Step over the place you've buried the paper, and that person will soon fade from your life.

Classic Candle Spell Of Love

- A pink candle
- Rose oil
- A little dried lavender or rose petals

Sprinkle the petals around and set your candle-holder on top. Rub the rose oil along the candle, and light it in the holder. Repeat the words:

I need to find love

I need it to last

I yearn to find love

Please let it come fast

Repeat the words 3 times, and then leave the candle to burn out. Watch for some new love to make itself known

The Confidence Candle

Improving your own opinion of yourself can go a long way in giving you confidence in any part of your life. This candle spell helps you learn to love yourself. All you need is:

- 1 Pink candle
- Some Pink and white rose petals
- Some Pure water

Any water will do but rainwater is best

On an altar or table, make a ring of flower petals and set up the candle in the center. Before you light it, think of your best traits and concentrate on those for a few minutes. Light the candle. Repeat the following:

> May my own light shine
>
> With love Divine

Take a long drink of water, to cleanse out your negative thoughts of yourself. Leave the candle to burn out on its own.

Personal Space Cleansing

Keep negative energy out of your space with a little candle spell. It is a suitable spell for one room, rather than your whole house. You'll need:

- Blue taper candle
- Square of white paper
- Salt

Lay the paper out on your altar or table, and set up the candle in the center of it. Use a clear glass candle-holder if you have one, though any type will do. Sprinkle a circle of salt around the paper, so that all 4 corners of the paper are just touching the salt.

Light the candle right at the top of the hour (exactly 1 o'clock, or 2 o'clock etc.), and let it burn right down. When it's done, carefully brush the salt onto the paper, and pour it down the drain. Bury the paper outside. All the bad energy in the room is now gone.

• • • • • • • • • •

Voodoo Spells

Passion At Your Door

Hot pepper can get things moving, and is used in lots of different Voodoo spells. I've already included this spell on another love spells page, but it really does belong here too. You should gather up:

- 3 drops hot pepper sauce
- 3 drops lavender oil
- Whole peppercorns
- Orris root pieces
- Rosemary
- 3 cups of rain water

The exact amount of herbs aren't important, as long as you have a little bit of each one in somewhat even proportions. Just a few pinches is fine. Pour everything together in a bowl and stir it around. Think about the heat of the peppers, and the passion you want to bring into your life.

Sprinkle the water around on your front doorstep, with your fingers. Not just the step, but flick your fingers to spray a bit on the frame and walkway as well (this may not work well if you live in an apartment). You don't necessarily have to use all the water, but don't be stingy with it either. It needs to be sprayed around, not just poured out.

When you are done, make sure to wash your hands. Even a little hot pepper sauce in the eyes will hurt.

Double Poppet

Poppets are common in many forms of Voodoo magic, and this spell will help you find the love of your life. You may have to search around a little for Adam and Eve root. Many online occult shops will carry it.

- 2 pieces of Adam and Eve root
- 1 black poppet
- 1 red poppet
- Catnip
- Vervain
- Red and black string or yarn

For the herbs, you just need a few pinches of each. You have to make a small felt or cloth figure that you can stuff, one in black and one in red. They don't need to be very large. As you make them, put one piece of Adam and Eve root in each one and some of the other herbs. Make sure they are sew tightly shut so the herbs don't leak out.

If you've added faces to your poppets, they need to be placed facing each other for this spell. Place the two poppets together, and tie them once with red yarn and once with black. Keep the knots tight. Place this charm on your windowsill during the night of the full moon, and leave it there until the next full moon. Love will soon come calling.

Lucky Floor Wash

Using a floor wash is a very common form of spell in Voodoo, so I figured that was a good place to start. This is a pretty general-purpose one to help bring good fortune to your home.

- Van Van oil
- A bucket of clean water

Follow the link above for a Van Van recipe before you begin. Add about 2 tablespoons of completed oil to a bucket of warm water. The exact measurements aren't that important. You should be able to smell the oil scent really lightly after you've mixed the wash.

Use a mop or sponge to wipe down a busy room in your house, like the kitchen or living room. Don't let anyone walk in the area until it is completely and thoroughly dry. This should bring some good fortune into your life within 7 days.

Paper Money Enchantment

You can bring a little extra cash into your life with this Voodoo spell for money. Gather up the following items:

- A piece of paper money
- Needle and red thread
- A piece of red cloth larger than the bill
- Coarse salt, at least a cup
- Pink candles
- Orange oil
- Amber incense

Gently use the needle and thread to sew the dollar bill onto the red cloth. Hang it up on wall, where you can set up the rest of your spell under it.

On a table or altar, sprinkle a thick line of salt to make a square. Set a candle at each corner and light them. Set a little open dish of orange oil in the center. Dip the end of your incense stick into the oil, then light it in a holder outside of the square. Repeat the words out loud:

Pinned to my life evermore

Accompany me to every shore

I trade you for different thing

Come back to my pockets bring

Leave the candles and incense burning for an hour, then snuff them out. Leaving everything set up, repeat the spell (lighting candles, incense, words) again for the next 2 days at the same time. Within 15 days, you should have some extra money.

Make Me Well Spell

I already have an herbal health poppet spell on the Spells for Healing page, but here is another example of a voodoo doll spell that can be used when you have an illness to fight. You need to have:

- Blue fabric
- A few handfuls of dried beans (any kind will do)
- 2 small white buttons
- Piece of white paper

Cut the fabric in 2 pieces that are roughly shaped like a person. Sew it up like the usual voodoo doll just making sure that the stitches are firm and tight because you'll be filling the doll with beans rather than soft stuffing.

Draw a cross on the paper and put it into the doll body along with the beans. Sew it up, and then fasten on the 2 white buttons where the eyes should be.

Keep the doll under your bed until your illness has passed.

The Stand Tall Doll

Ok, a little silly with the name of this poppet spell but it's a spell to help you gain some courage and confidence. Bring some additional strength to your life with a few simple supplies:

- 3 sticks, about 6 to 8 inches long
- Heavy twine or rough string
- 1 sturdy nail
- 1 dried chili pepper

Actual branches or twigs are best for this spell, but you can use dowels or even Popsicle sticks if that's what you have on hand.

Use the twine to tie the sticks together in a rough A shape, with the cross-piece close to the top to create a shape that looks like a person (well, it has 2 arms and 2 legs anyway).

Tie the chili pepper to one leg and the nail to the other. Wrap all the limbs and head of your stick doll in twine a few more times. Stand the doll upright somewhere important in your home where you will frequently see it. When you do, remind yourself to stand tall when you make your choices during the day.

Pour On Protection

A strong protection spell with voodoo elements, to be used to block unwanted magick from coming into your home. Do this spell on the night of the new moon (the dark moon). You'll need to have:

A cups of pure water (rain is best)

Black ink

4 or 5 black whole peppercorns

A pinch of graveyard dirt

A splash of vodka

1 red candle

Light the candle before you begin. Mix everything together in a bowl made from glass, metal or ceramic. Stir everything around with the index finger of your left hand. Call to the voodoo God Legba to protect your house.

Go out to your front door, and pour the mixture all over the steps or walkway coming up to the door. Splash it around good. You can continually refresh the spell by pouring out a new shot of vodka over the same area each night of the new moon.

Floor Wash Lover

Floor washes may seem like a strange way to do magick, but it's a very common spell format in voodoo and hoodoo. Here is a recipe for making a floor wash to help bring a little new love into your life.

1 quart of fresh rain water (clean stream water would do)

Half a fresh lime

5 drops of pure rose oil

1 whole bay leaf

Several whole white mustard seeds

Mix everything together and let it "steep" for at least an hour. After that, get on your hands and knees and wash the floor in your kitchen with this mixture. You don't need to scrub or anything like that, just rub down the entire floor. It will start to draw love for you as soon as the floor dries.

Mop On The Luck

Using a floor wash is a very common form of spell in Voodoo, so I figured that was a good place to start. This is a pretty general-purpose one to help bring good fortune to your home.

- Van Van oil
- A bucket of clean water

Follow the link above for a Van Van recipe before you begin. Add about 2 tablespoons of completed oil to a bucket of warm water. The exact measurements aren't that important. You should be able to smell the oil scent really lightly after you've mixed the wash.

Use a mop or sponge to wipe down a busy room in your house, like the kitchen or living room. Don't let anyone walk in the area until it is completely and thoroughly dry. This should bring some good fortune into your life within 7 days.

Doll Of Romance

This is a doll spell that is used to make someone to fall in love with you. Wiccans or other Pagans may not appreciate this style of magic, but it is perfectly acceptable within Voodoo.

- A doll to represent your desired partner
- Something from him or her
- Similar items from yourself
- 3 lengths of ribbon, in red, black and white
- Paper
- 1 Pen or marker with red ink
- 1 white candle

The doll can be carved from wax, molded from clay or sewn from fabric. A hand-made doll is much more powerful than a store-bought object, so take the time to do it right. Add in the items from their body, using hairs, nail clippings or at least a bit of fabric from clothes they have worn. Also use the same items from yourself. Write or carve his/her name into the doll as well.

Perform this spell on the day after the new moon. Set up your altar and light the candle. Wrap the doll in each piece of ribbon, knotting each one when necessary to keep it attached. Say out loud:

Ribbons bind and entwine

Your heart, forever linked to mine

Write your beloved's name on the paper and leave it on the altar. Set the doll on the paper and snuff out the candle. The next night, light the candle again and pick up the doll.

Very lightly and very carefully run the feet of the doll near the flame, and say:

For you, I yearn

For me, you burn

Again, set the doll on the paper. This time, leave the candle burning for at least an hour. The person you want will soon show some interest in you and quickly fall in love. When your spell is successful, wrap up the doll and put it somewhere safe to keep the attraction going.

Love Root

This variation on a rootwork spell will draw someone to you for some loving. It's particularly potent if you're after added passion as well as romance. You'll need:

- A large piece of St. John the Conquerer root
- Black thread
- Red thread
- Strands of your hair
- Strands of your subject's hair
- A Ceramic dish filled with dirt
- 1 red candle

Yes, it can be difficult to get some strands of another person's hair, and yes you still have to do it.

Wrap the piece of root with the hair, and then wrap further with the red and black thread. Use enough thread to really secure the hair in place. Set the tied root charm in the bowl, and cover it over with dirt.

Light the red candle and hold it over the dish. Let several big drops of red wax drop onto the dirt over the root, then set the candle back up in a candle holder and let it continue burning.

After 1 week, your desired partner will start to show some serious interest in you.

Light Up Your Love

- Red candles in the shape of a man and a woman

"Come to Me" oil

A large red dish or platter to hold both candles (not separate holders)

Human shaped candles aren't too easy to find, but most occult or Pagan shops should carry them. You can also use 2 female or 2 male if that is what you need. If your local shop doesn't carry Come to Me oil, use a mix of patchouli and vanilla oils with a pinch of saffron.

Use something sharp to write your name in the wax of one candle, and the subject of your spell in the other. If you aren't after anyone particular, write "my beloved" instead.

Anoint both candles in the oil, and set them up in a large dish. They should be close enough to touch. Light the candle representing you first, and then the other one. Simply say "By the power of all the Saints, bring me my love" and leave the candles to burn out.

• • • • • • • • •

White Magic

Travel Charmed

Not only will this charm bag keep you safe when you are away from home, it will keep you from getting lost. Of course, that doesn't mean you shouldn't bring a map along with you. You need the following items:

• A small piece of red cloth (flannel is best)

• Dirt

• Several large pieces of rock salt

• A small piece of real silver (coin, ring, bead)

Sew the cloth into a little bag, and fill with the other items. Sew the bag shut, and keep it with you when you travel

Peaceful Sleeping

The right blend of herbs can do wonders for a good night's sleep. This sachet spell can help you have a more restful sleep and keep your dreams positive.

- 10 whole cardamom pods
- 1 tbs sea salt
- 15 whole cloves
- 1/2 oz dried mint
- 1/2 oz dried rosemary
- 1 white candle
- 1 pink candle
- 1 silver candle
- 1 small bag or pouch

Light all three candles wherever you are going to be working on your herbal pouch. In a small bowl, mix everything together with your hands. Keep your thoughts peaceful while you work. You should do this spell in a quiet moment when you won't be disturbed.

Repeat this chant while you stir your fingers through the herbs:

Sleep.. dream.. peace

Peace.. dream.. sleep

Dream.. sleep   peace

Pour the herbs into the bag, and tie it closed. Set is somewhere near your bed. You can sleep with it under your pillow, but it will be quite aromatic and lumpy

Threshold Defence Spell

This is a simple spell to help keep negative energy and/or spirits from getting into your house. All you need is:

- 3 cloves of garlic
- A handful of coarse sea salt
- A handful of rosemary

Stir everything together in a bowl, and leave on a windowsill during the night of a full moon. Hopefully it will be a clear night so the moonlight can touch your spell materials.

Then take the bowl outside, and spread the salt and herbs around the outside of your front door and any other doors in the house. The main door that you use should get the most of the mixture. For added protection, sprinkle a little on the window sills too.

If you live in an apartment, this spell can still be performed but the garlic smell will be noticeable if you sprinkle too much on your door to the hallway.

Bottle Of Cash

This is a personal favorite that has worked well for me on more than one occasion. You will need a few items for this spell though:

- 1 small bottle with a lid
- 5 coins in different denominations
- 5 kernels of dried corn
- 5 sesame seeds
- 5 pieces of cinnamon stick
- 5 whole cloves
- 5 allspice seeds
- 5 peanuts

Choose a bottle large enough to fit everything but not too large. You want to fill the bottle. And the peanuts are just the edible parts (no shells) and unsalted.

Put everything in the bottle and shake it up. While you're doing so, repeat the words of the spell:

> Silver & spices
>
> Copper & grain
>
> Help me increase
>
> My financial gain

Store the finished bottle near where you keep your wallet or purse, but you don't have to carry it with

The Four Elements Of Wealth

This spell for money uses energy from all four elements for some added power. It's still a very simple spell that only takes a few minutes. Your supplies are:

- Salt
- Water
- 1 green candle
- Sage incense

Light the incense and say: May air blow riches towards me

Light the candle and say: May fire light my way

Put some salt on your tongue, and say: May earth grow my fortune

Drink the water and say: May water cleanse me today

Leave the incense and candle to burn out. Leave a little bit of each element on your altar until your money troubles are over. So, leave the candle stub, incense ash and small bowls of both salt and water. Refill the water as necessary

Free Yourself From Stress

For this spell, you need the following supplies:

- 1 red candle
- 1 white candle
- Lavender oil
- Cinnamon oil
- Piece of red jasper
- Piece of clear quartz

Place the red candle in front of you , and anoint it with the cinnamon oil. Light it, and think of all the things that currently stress you out. Hold the red jasper in your hand, and let all the stressful things pour out of your mind and into the stone.

Move the lit candle farther away from you, and set the stone at the base. Then bring the white candle to you, and rub with lavender oil. Light the candle. Now think peaceful thoughts and focus on being relaxed and stress-free.

Leave both candles to burn down, and take the piece of clear quartz with you to remind you to leave the stress behind.

Hook-Up With A Friend Spell

Try a little magick spell to have a friend get in touch again. You will need these items:

- A white candle
- Sandalwood oil and incense
- Photograph of your friend
- Glass bowl or cup of water
- Small handful of raw sea salt

Light your incense, and anoint the candle with the sandalwood oil. Light the candle to begin your spell. Set the photo in front of you and think about some of the memories you have of your friend. If you don't have a picture, write their full name on a piece of paper instead.

Slowly pour the salt into your bowl of water while you repeat, "Contact me" while the salt drops. Leave the bowl of salted water next to the candle while it burns. Your friend will make contact with you before the water evaporates from the bowl.

Tonka Bean Token

Tonka beans are traditionally used for money-drawing spellwork and don't require much additional magick to turn them into money talismans. All you need is:

• One whole tonka bean

Yep, that's it. Though you might have to do a little searching for a tonka bean. Occult shops or herb suppliers should have them.

Hold the bean in your hand and repeat the following:

I have a tonka bean

Because times are lean

May it draw me money

Like bees to honey

Carry the bean around everywhere you go, and like with the last spell, a purse is best. It needs to stay near where you carry your money when you

Seeds of Passion

You'll need to get these items together:

- 9 sunflower seeds
- 9 dried beans
- 9 dry kernels of corn
- 9 grains of barley
- 9 dry chamomile buds
- 9 whole cloves
- Rose oil
- Glass bottle with stopper
- Red ribbon

You need to choose a bottle that will hold all the seeds, but won't have too much empty space at the top either. This Wiccan love spell should be performed on the night of the new moon.

Drop each of the seeds into the bottle, one by one. Yes, it's a bit tedious but that's how it's done. As you do so, repeat the following lines:

>Seeds and spices, give me power
>
>Time to make my love life flower

As the moon grows in the sky

This charm will make my wishes fly

When the bottle is filled, add 9 drops of rose oil to the top and stopper it up. Don't shake, you need to let the oil work its way down from the top. Tie the red ribbon in a bow around the bottle and place it somewhere quiet where it won't be disturbed. By the full moon, you should see some action in the love department.

Passion on Your Doorstep

The use of hot pepper in love spells is kind of a Voodoo tradition, but can be pretty successful in any kind of spellwork. Get your ingredients together:

- 3 drops hot pepper sauce
- 3 cups of rain water
- Dried rosemary
- Black peppercorns
- Dried orris root pieces
- 3 drops Lavender oil

You don't need to be too precise with the herbs. Two or three pinches of each would be fine, just try to use the same amount for all the herbs. Stir everything together in a bowl, while you concentrate on drawing love and passion into your life.

Using your fingers, sprinkle the mixture around your front doorstep. Don't just pour it all out in one spot. Wash your hands well afterwards, and wait for love to come knocking at your door.

Charm of the Oak

This spell is a way to connect to the deep wisdom and knowledge embodied in the oak tree. It's a more spiritual and somewhat intangible spell than most others. All you need is:

- 4 acorns
- Small bag of brown fabric
- Patchouli oil
- A brown or green candle

Best if you can collect the acorns yourself. Anoint the candle and the acorns with oil, and light the candle. While you hold the acorns in your hands, repeat the following: Sacred oak

Blessed seed

Growth and wisdom

Mine indeed Visualize a mighty oak tree, and all the things it may have to teach you. Place the acorns in the bag, and leave it near the candle. Let the candle burn out on its own, and leave the bag somewhere where you will see it every day. Opportunities to gain new knowledge will soon present themselves.

Fertility Spell

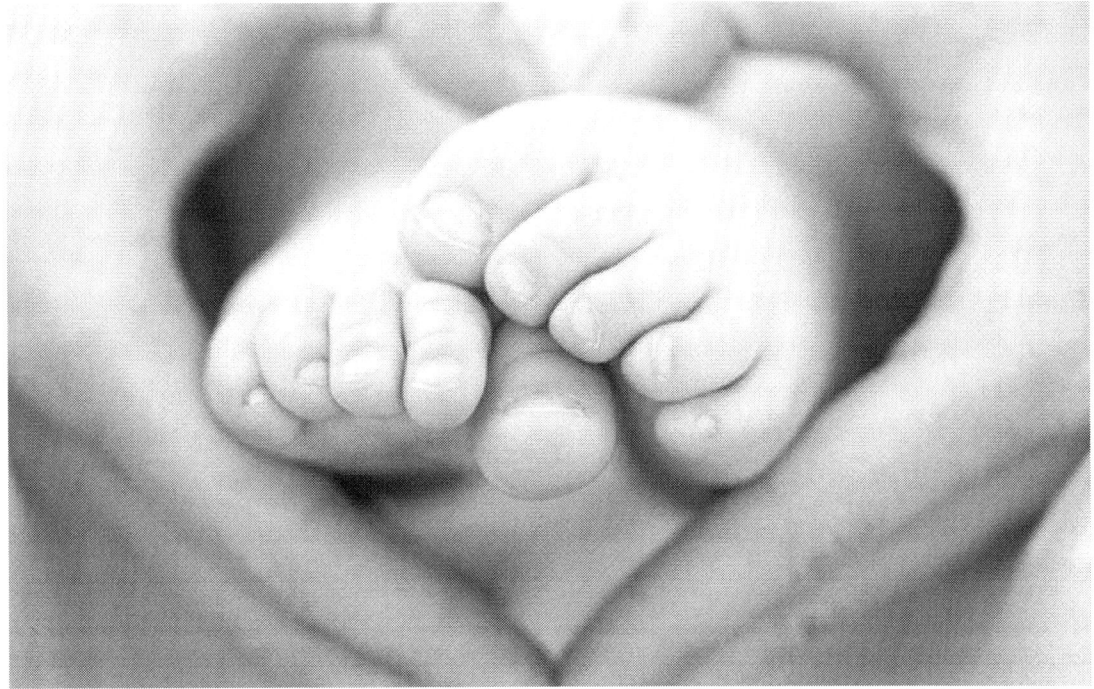

A little magic can help in your quest to become pregnant, but don't be foolish and ignore any possible medical issues. Your supplies for this earth spell are just:

- 1 raw egg
- 1 whole vanilla bean
- 1 Pencil

Write these symbols on an egg. They're in Theban script, and read "ripe". Go outside and dig a hole in your yard, and bury the egg with the vanilla bean. Make sure it's deep enough that an animal won't dig it up. If you don't have a yard, use a large flower pot filled with earth.

This spell works best if you bury the egg during a waxing moon, though you don't necessarily have to do it at night. Each night afterwards though, you have to go outside and water the spot so your spell can "grow".

Lemon Love

This particular love spell is designed to bring back your ex, and is pretty easy to do.

You'll need:

- A fresh lemon
- A little piece of paper (pink if you have it)

A length of red yarn or ribbon

On the piece of paper, write your name and your ex's name then slice open the lemon. Try to cut it evenly in half. Fold the paper so the names are touching, and sandwich is between the lemon pieces. Tie the red yarn around the lemon to hold it together. As you do all of this, visualize you getting your ex back and how happy that would make you.

Now put the little lemon bundle in the freezer (yes, the freezer) and tuck it in the back so nobody can see it. You can expect to see your ex back in your life in a month.

Midsummer Rose

You might have to be pretty determined to get your ex back, because there is only one day a year when it will work. Hopefully Midsummer's eve (June 20th) isn't too far away when you need this spell. It's actually a pretty easy spell, but might mean a little legwork (especially if you live in a big city).

To be clear, Midsummer is the longest day of the year and usually falls on either the 20th or 21st of June. Midsummer eve is the evening before.

For this spell you need:

- 5 red roses
- Tree that contains a bird's nest
- A church
- Natural running water, like a stream
- A crossroads

You can pick out your locations beforehand, but you must do everything on Midsummer's Eve. Bury a rose under the tree, set one near the gate of the church, another near running water and another one where 2 roads cross. The last rose goes under your own pillow. Sleep with it there for 3 nights. On the fourth night, pluck the petals from that rose, and leave a few of them at the 4 locations where you left the first roses. You'll get your ex back before you know it.

Silver Ring Lover

One particularly powerful way to cast a love spell, is to bless an item as a charm and wear it near you after the spell is cast. For this spell, you will create a charm out of a ring, though it will take a month to complete. You'll need the following items for this spell:

- A silver ring that you have never worn before
- A white cloth
- A cup of white wine

You need to perform this spell under the light of a full moon, so hopefully the skies will be clear for you or you should wait for another night.

Wrap the ring in the cloth, and bury it under ground. Sit quietly and watch the moon as you concentrate on the qualities you are seeking in a new love relationship. Pour the wine over the spot where you burying the ring, and recite the spell:

- Sacred Goddess, fair and true
- A silver gift I offer you
- Bless this ring and make it shine
- Bring a lover to be mine

Leave the ring for a month, and dig it up on the next full moon. From that day on, wear it every day to attract your true love to you

Key to Your Heart Spell

This is a very easy love spell that will take you very little time to perform though it will be 2 weeks before the charm is finished. You will need the following items:

- 3 candles (gold, silver and red)
- 2 red roses
- 1 horseshoe

- 1 key
- 1 red silk scarf

This is a spell for a Friday night (like most love spells). Light all three candles on your altar, and wrap the roses, horseshoe and key in the silk scarf. Pass the bundle through the heat of the candle flames, ideally without it all catching on fire. Put it in your underwear drawer for 2 weeks. Yes, your underwear drawer.

After the 2 weeks are up, bury the roses outside and keep the horseshoe and key someplace safe near your bed. They will draw a new love to you within a month.

Fairy Bells

This spell should be done at night, with the intention of asking the fairies for some magical good luck. Your supplies are:

- 1 small silver bell
- 1 white candle
- Rose oil

Anoint the candle with rose oil, and announce that you are going to ask the fairies for their blessings. Ring the bell three times and say:

> When the bell rings, my spirit sings
>
> I summon the fairies of light
>
> To bless me with their magic this night

Ring the bell for another 3 times, and say the words again. Repeat one more time and then go to bed. Leave the candle burning some where safe. In the morning, ring the bell one single time and thank the fairies.

Find a Fairy

You will need the following items:

- A pretty glass bottle, fairly small with a stopper
- Enough rain water to fill the bottle
- Rose petals
- Lavender blossoms
- 3 small pieces of quartz
- 3 small pieces of amethyst
- A sprinkle of sugar
- A drop of vanilla extract
- 1 Pink ribbon

Fill up your bottle with all the ingredients except for the pink ribbon. Tie the pink ribbon around the neck of the bottle, in a nice bow. After the sun goes down, go outside to a wooded area. If you can find an oak tree or a patch of mushrooms, all the better. Your own yard is best, or a secluded area. Fairies don't usually take up residence in busy public parks.

Dab a couple drops of the fairy potion in the bottle on your wrists, and stopper the bottle back up. Place the bottle under the tree or wherever you've decided is the best place to find a fairy. Sit next to the bottle, and repeat the following:

Let me see a fairy today

A little one, fly my way

Gentle wings for little things

Sacred, magical, fairy flight

Repeat for 3 times total. Then sit very still and you might catch some movement out of the corner of your eye. Leave the bottle as an offering to the little folks, which might bring greater success next time you try this spell. They will remember a pretty gift.

Storm Enchantment

If you are hoping for exciting weather, this spell can help you conjure up a storm. You only need a few things:

- A sprig of broom
- Sea salt
- Water
- A Wooden spoon
- A red candle

Now, for this spell you need a piece of the broom plant, NOT an actual broom you sweep with. You may have to check herb suppliers, florists or plants shops to find it. There really isn't a substitute for broom in a weather spell.

Light the red candle and pour water into the bowl while you say:

Rain that brings a land's rebirth

Time to weep upon the earth.

Use the spoon to stir up the water, then dip the piece of broom in. Repeat:

Winds will follow, you shall see

Blowing wildly through the trees

Envision a storm growing in strength and power. Let a few drops of hot wax from the candle fall into the water, and say:

Lightning quick, lightning long

Make it last, make it strong

Add in the salt to seal the spell and stir again. Give it one last stir, and take it immediately outside and toss it all into the air (you can hold on to the bowl). Don't let the water settle down before you throw it. Now you can expect a storm to start brewing on the horizon within a few days.

Sunny Skies Enchantment

And for the other side of the weather coin, here is a spell to bring in some sunny skies. All you need is:

- A very small bowl
- Enough rainwater to fill the bowl
- Salt
- Yellow or orange candle

The size of the bowl kind of depends on when you want the sunny weather to kick in, so choose a dish after reading the whole spell. Fill the bowl with rainwater, and add a few pinches of salt. Not coarse sea salt, but regular fine-ground salt. Set the bowl in a window sill, or on a table near the window. Place the candle nearby and light it. Repeat the following:

Rain, rain go away

Come back another day

Yes the words are a bit cliche, but they do sum up your intentions nicely. Let the candle burn for at least an hour, or let it burn until it's done on its own. The weather will start to clear up as the water evaporates from the bowl. When the dish is dry, it will be bright and sunny out again.

Spring Garden Spell

A garden is already a pretty magickal place, but a little spellwork can help your plants thrive. This spell is meant for the early spring when plants are just starting to sprout. You will need:

- 1 pint of milk
- A few spoons of honey
- 4 wooden garden stakes
- A length of green ribbon

If you can get organic milk and honey, even better. Mix the honey into the milk, and bring it out side to your garden with the stakes and ribbon. Try to do this on a sunny day after your plants have begun to come up.

Cut your ribbon into 4 pieces, long enough to tie a bow around the tops of each stake. Choose 4 points around your garden that would more or less surround the plants. North, south, east and west are ideal but not necessary. At each point, pour some of the honey milk and then push the stake into the moist earth. With each stake, say:

> Milk and honey, flowing out
>
> Goddess bless my every sprout
>
> Growing strong
>
> Season's long
>
> Today I bless my garden

Your garden is now blessed with magic, but you still need to water it regularly and keep it free of weeds if you want it to thrive.

Cool Your Anger

Does your temper sometimes get the best of you? Take a few minutes to perform this easy spell to you help keep a cool head. Your supplies are:

- A few spoonfuls of mint leaves
- Tablespoon or more of honey
- Water and a teacup

Heat the water to just boiling, and pour over the mint leaves. Take a few deep breaths and inhale the aroma of the mint as it steeps. Let your anger evaporate along with the steam. Strain out the leaves and add honey to the tea.

Let it cool a bit, and drink. As you enjoy your mint tea, repeat the following a few times:

>Cool my mind, leaves of mint
>
>Honey, sweeten my intent
>
>My attitude has to change
>
>Anger must go out of range

This should help you cool off, and see the situation in a better perspective. Sit quietly until the entire cup of tea is finished.

• • • • • • • • •

Black Magic Spells

Bad Luck Lock

This is a pretty generic bad luck spell to put on someone when you don't have anything in particular in mind. All you'll need is:

A solid padlock (keyed, not combination)

A sheet of paper

Something sharp like a pointed screwdriver

Black paint

Write a person's name on a piece of paper and fold it over once. Pierce the paper through the center to make a hole. Don't use a hole punch, it has to be pierced with something pointed. Put the hasp of the lock through the hole and lock the lock.

Brush a glob of black paint over the keyhole and on either side of the lock. Hold the lock by the hasp until it dries, while repeating the following:

Blackest lock

Blackest luck

By this spell,

You now are stuck.

Now bury the lock somewhere in your yard, bury the key as close to your target's home as possible. If you don't know where they live, bury it your own yard, but not near the lock.

The Dead of Night

This is a real black magic spell specifically to bring nightmares to another person. You should cast this spell after midnight but before dawn, and be aware that it will make a bit of smoke. Have a window handy. You need:

A black candle

Mugwort

Dragon's blood resin

Charcoal tablet

Heat-proof dish

Large piece of white paper or cloth

Black ink (a marker will do)

On the paper or cloth, drawn 3 concentric circles and an x in the center. Set up the dish and charcoal on the x, and the candle outside the circles. Light the charcoal and get it smoldering, put a pinch or two of mugwort on it along with a chunk of resin. When they are both smoking, light the candle.

Watch the smoke rising from the dish and visualize it floating through space to your intended target. It brings nightmares and fear into their sleep, and picture that scene for several minutes and focus on the person.

After a few minutes, put out the charcoal and switch the dish and candle so the candle is on the x. Leave it until it fully burns down. Your victim will have bad dreams starting the next night and it will last for 3 days.

Sweet Apple Enchantment

Don't all good black magic spells include a lock of hair? Well, that's because it's a powerful way to connect another person to your spell. Your supplies for this ritual:

- **1 apple, preferably a red one**
- **Honey**
- **A few strands of your hair**
- **A few strands of your intended lover's hair**
- **Length of red ribbon or yarn**

Slice the apple sideways across the middle, so you can see the star formed by the seeds. Spread honey on either half of the apple. Take the strands of hair, and twist or braid them together.

Put the hairs between the two halves, and tie the apple back together with the ribbon. Tie it tightly. Bury the apple either outside, or in a large flower pot (outside is best). You'll find your desired lover start to show a strong interest in you almost immediately. love spells

Your Heart be Mine

Turn someone's heart towards you while you completely immerse yourself in this black magic love spell. You'll only need a few things:

- 2 pink candles
- 2 white candles
- Piece of paper
- Red marker
- Jasmine or Ylang Ylang oil

Before you begin, run yourself a hot bath. At the 4 corners of the tub, light the candles.

Then on the piece of paper, draw a large heart in marker and put your name and your intended lover's name in the center. Draw a larger heart around the first one (after the names are written in).

Rub a drop of oil into each corner of the paper, then fold into quarters. Hold the folded paper in your hands and repeat the two names out loud several times. Don't unfold the paper, and tear it into small pieces. Drop the pieces into the bath water.

Now you get in the tub. Stir the water around to help dissolve the paper, and rub the pieces on your body while you soak. Stay in the tub until the paper is completely broken down in the water.

Joining Of Two Photo Spell

If you want your potential lover to be stuck on you, this is the best of the black magic love spells. The photos you use shouldn't have anyone else in them except for you and him/her. Supplies for this spell:

- Photo of you
- Photo of the one you desire
- Red candle
- Pen or marker

On the back of the picture of him/her, write "I love you" and on the back of your photo, write "You love me". Light the candle and look at both photos, picturing the two of you together in real life. Drip candle wax on the front sides of both photos and quickly stick them together.

Repeat the following:

Slip the pair of photos under your pillow, and sleep with them there until your loved one is yours.

Raging Boil

Boiling water will help you harness your emotional energy into a potent little curse charm.

Cooking pot

About a cup of water

A few tablespoons of raw rock salt

A dead flower blossom (any kind)

A small jar or vial with a stoppered lid

Get the water boiling on the stove, and toss in the salt (save at least one piece for later). Repeat the following:

Heat and power

This dead flower

By this curse,

I make it worse

Drop in the flower. Repeat the words again, this time saying your victim's name three times at the end. Repeat again.

curse spells

Watch the water boil and feel your own anger bubbling inside of you. Direct that energy into your spell, and then leave the pot to boil for a few more minutes. Do not let it boil dry! Take the pot off the heat, and pour the hot water into your bottle. Let it cool down and drop in another bit of salt. Seal up the bottle. Repeat the spell words again, including the name of your target.

Keep the bottle somewhere safe until the curse has worked its magick.

Belladonna Bottle

Herbal magick can be a good source of curse spells, though finding some belladonna may not be that simple because it is poisonous. And yes, this is another bottle spell. I'm just on a roll that way right now.

- Dried belladonna
- A black candle
- Metal filings or flakes of rust
- A small bottle
- A single sewing needle

Light the black candle and watch the flame for a few minutes while the wax starts to melt. Focus your thoughts on your target and why you want to place this curse spell on them.

Put some bits of rust or metal in the bottom of the bottle along with the belladonna, and then drop in the sewing needle.

When the wax has started melting pick up the candle and drip some into the bottle. Try to fill it at least a third full (use a small bottle to keep it simple). It should cover over all the contents to keep it in place, though the sewing needle can still stick out of the wax. Say the words, "Poison you" five times and put the lid on the bottle.

Bury the charm in your yard and it should start to work in a few days.

Covet Candle

Do you know someone who has something you want? This is a spell designed to make them lose it and have it come to you instead. It's not a love spell to "take" a person though, this is for objects only.

And it may not work in a literal sense. If you want their TV, they can lose theirs through damage or theft and then you find yourself with extra money to buy your own. You don't always get their item exactly. You get the idea. It depends on the situation.

Your supplies for this spell include:

- A dark green candle
- Hot red pepper flakes
- Two images of the object you want
- A fire-proof dish

You can use photos from newspapers or magazine, or make a drawing yourself. It doesn't have to be an exact photo of the actual object. Just a representation.

Put the two images together, face to face, with a sprinkling of red pepper flakes between them. Fold the pages in half, and then in half again. Make sure the flakes stay inside the paper. Repeat the following:

I covet and seek,

To take from the meek.

Bring this to me,

I wish it to be.

Visualize the person you wish to take the object from, and light the paper bundle on fire in the dish. Before it burns out completely, use the flames to light the candle. Repeat the words again, focusing on the object and the person who has it.

Leave the candle to burn out on its own. You should time this spell so that some part of it is still going at midnight, even if its just the candle burning.

Sickness Descends

This is a spell to bring illness down on someone. You can use this kind of dark magic spell as a form of revenge, or to get someone out of the way when competing for something in your life (romance, a job, an actual competition).

- A rotten egg
- A photo or drawing of the person
- Wood ash
- A rusted pin or nail

Odds of having a rotten egg just sitting around are pretty slim, so you should plan on doing this spell in advance. Leave a whole (uncracked) raw egg out in the sun for several days until is starts to smell a little ripe. It can take a week or even more.

When you are ready to do this spell (try for a Saturday), remember that it will smell bad and you might not want other people home when you do it.

Set out the photo on a table, on a plate or tray. Puncture the egg with the rusted pin and crack it open over the photo. Let the gunk cover up the picture as you think about that person getting sick. Sprinkle wood ash over the rotten egg. Let everything sit for a few minutes. Again, concentrate on your intentions as you enjoy the aroma.

Then take the plate outside, and bury the whole mess with the photo facing downwards. Your target will be ill within a week.

Reflect and Revenge

Mirrors are very powerful for returning energy back to someone, and are perfect for revenge spells like this. You'll need a few supplies:

- A small mirror
- Black permanent marker
- Long piece of black ribbon
- Whole bay leaf
- Burnt wood ash

If you can, cast this spell on a Saturday night. First write the person's name on the face of the mirror is big letters, then set the bay leaf over the name. Wrap the mirror and leaf in ribbon a few times, then add a generous pinch of ash over the leaf. Wrap a few more times and then tie with a solid knot.

Place one hand on either side of the mirror, and say:

From me to you,

Comes back times two.

Keep the wrapped up mirror charm under your bed, until you feel that your revenge has taken place. Don't leave it forever though. Once some bad luck has fallen on your adversary, remove it and dismantle the spell.

Black Moon Vengeance

Check the calendar for the next new moon, and plan to do this dark spell on that night. All you need is:

- 1 black candle
- Sharp tool to scribe the candle
- Piece of onyx or jet

Carve the name of your target into the candle and set it into a candle holder. Focus on the wrong this person did to you, and watch the flame burn. When the candle has melted down enough to start melting where you wrote their name, take it out of the holder and drop several drips of melting wax over the stone.

While the wax is still soft, mark the person's first initial into the wax then let it cool and harden. Let the candle finish burning down, and leave the stone in a safe place (but out of sight) until your revenge has occurred. After that, bury the stone in the earth to end the spell.

Pepper Pentacle

This is a general spell to cause bad luck or misfortune to fall on someone. All you need is:

- White piece of paper
- Black pepper
- Pen

Black candle

Draw a pentacle on the paper, fairly large. Write your target's name in the center. Carefully sprinkle a fine line of pepper around the outline of the pentacle. Once done, light the candle and let it burn for a few minutes to get the wax melting.

Hold the candle over the pentacle and let several drops of wax fall on the person's name. Ideally, enough to cover the words. Then let the candle burn for an hour before putting it out. Leave your pepper sigil in place where it won't be disturbed until your spell has its effect.

Rocky Road Curse

This is an easy bad luck spell that you can use to target anyone in your life, even if you don't have any details about them.

- A rough rock, about the size of your fist
- Black paint
- Slip of paper
- Length of black yarn or ribbon
- A whole dry bay leaf

Paint the rock black, and let it completely dry before you continue with this spell.

Write your intended target's name on the piece of paper. If you don't know their name, describe them ("my noisy neighbor" or something like that). Fold the paper over once and tie it to the rock along with the bay leaf. The paper should be against the stone. Tie the string or whatever you're using in a strong knot.

Set the stone in a dark place so that it's sitting on the piece of paper. Give the spell 3 days to start to take effect, and your chosen person will start having quite a run of bad luck.

Snake Eyes Curse

Unexpected bad luck will show up for someone after doing this spell. The results are usually just one or two larger incidents of bad luck, rather than an ongoing streak (like the spell above).

- A pair of dice
- Black pepper
- Access to outside

Dig a hole several inches deep. Set the dice in the bottom, with the 1s facing upward. Cover them over with pepper and repeat the following:

Your luck has run out,

You're in a hole.

Bad things will happen,

That's my goal.

Concentrate on the person you are sending this spell to, and then fill the hole in with dirt. Stomp on it good and hard to tamp it down, then just leave it to make its magick.

Embrace the Darkness

Get in touch with your darker side with this night ritual, performed on the night of a new moon. You'll need the following:

- A dark bowl
- Black ink
- A sharp pin
- Black pepper
- 1 black candle

On the night of a new moon the sky is dark, and the perfect time to tap into your darker energies. Light the candle, but place it as far away from you as you can, but you should still be able to see what you're doing at your altar. The point is to work in shadow.

Fill the bowl with water, then add 9 drops of black ink. Wait for a few moments for the darkness to spread through the water. Sprinkle pepper on the surface of the water. Just a pinch is enough.

Now repeat the words of the shadow spell:

Shadows of darkness, spirits within

Harness the energy, let it begin

Draw down the moon

Bring me the shadows

I am ready to see

My other side

At this point, prick your finger with the pin and let a drop of blood fall into the water. Repeat the words a second time. Take the bowl outside and dump it all out into the Earth. You'll soon start to feel new connection to your darker shadow spirit.

Shaddow Speaks

This is a bit of a summoning spell, to address the very nature of the shadow.

- A large mirror
- A piece of black cloth large enough to cover the mirror
- Patchouli incense
- Black marker or paint

Use the marker or paint to draw the Theban symbols shown here in the 4 corners of the mirror. Lean your forehead to touch the center of the mirror for a few seconds, feeling the cold of the glass. Light the incense and drape fabric over the mirror.

Touch each of the 4 corners and then immediately rip away the cloth. In that instant, you'll get a strong impression or even see a message in the mirror from the shadow. It's a message you need right now but it may not be clear.

• • • • • • • • •

Protection Spells

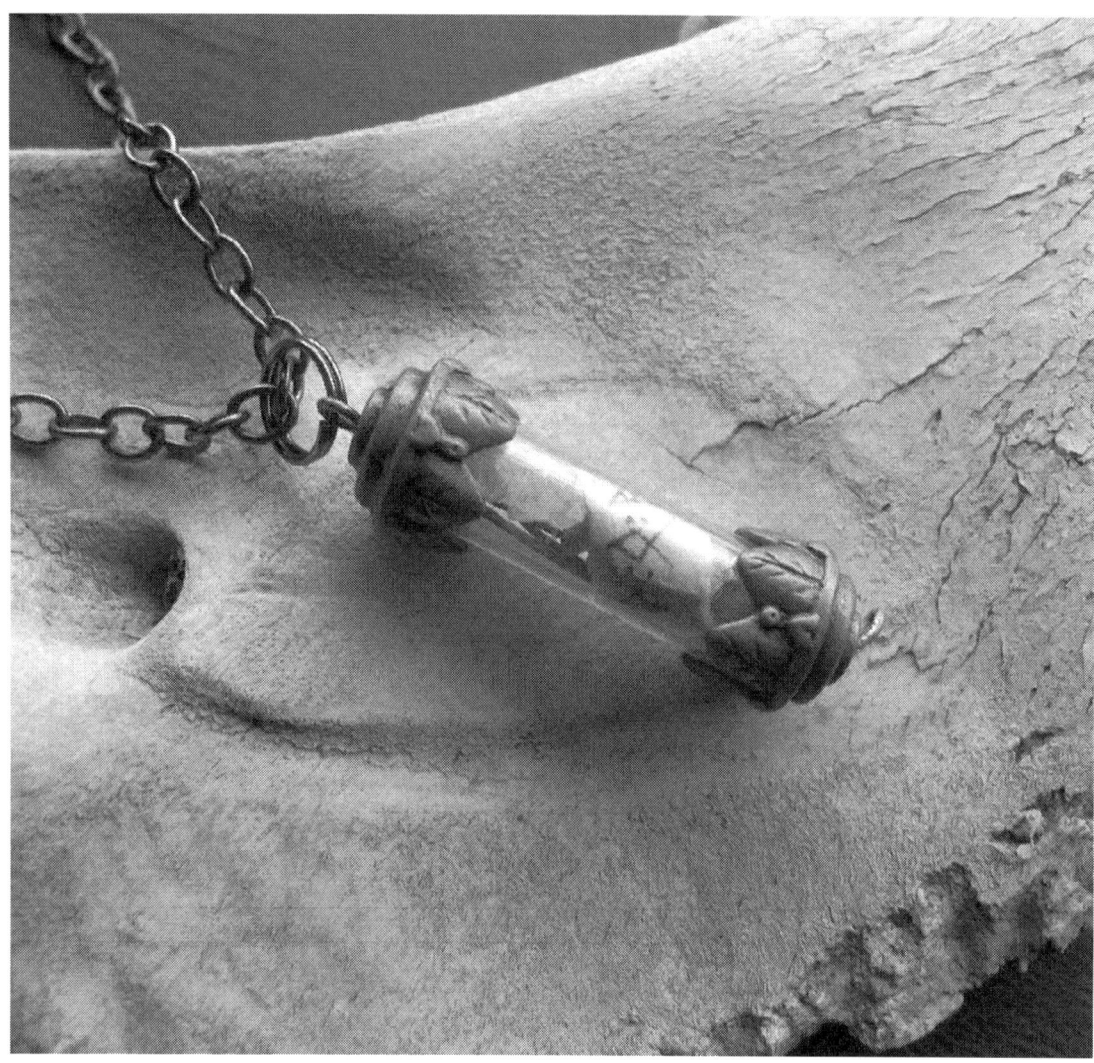

Banishing Mirror

This spell directs someone's vision back towards themselves, making you invisible to them. Not literally of course. For this spell, you will need:

- A small mirror
- Photo or drawing of the person
- Piece of onyx

- A pinch of mugwort

Place the mirror flat on a table, and sprinkle a pinch of mugwort in one spot on the face of the mirror. Lay the photo face-down on the mirror so the face of the person is over the mugwort. Repeat the following words:

> You cannot see me
>
> You cannot hear me
>
> You do not want me
>
> Now let me be

Now set the piece of onyx on top of the photo, also over where the persons face is (or as close as you can get since the photograph is lying upside down at this point).

Repeat the words again, and leave the items on your altar to keep this person away. For the most powerful effect, cast this banishing spell on the night of the new moon.

Frozen Enemy

Another classic banishing technique is to freeze someone to make them powerless against you. You just need:

- A small piece of paper
- A black pen
- A small piece of black string
- Water
- A freezer

On the piece of paper, write the name of the person you want to banish. Tie a single knot in the middle of the string, and concentrate on why this person is bothering you when you tie it.

Fold the paper up, with the piece of string tucked in the middle. Add a few drops of water to the paper. Don't soak it. You don't want to obliterate the name inside. Just dampen it enough that it will freeze solid. Place the wet folded paper in the freezer and leave there until the situation is passed.

The Banishing Jar

Let someone be annoying or difficult in their own world, and stay away from you. Your supplies for this spell are:

- A photo or drawing of the person
- A pin
- Vinegar
- Salt
- Jar with lid

If you are using a drawing, write the person's name on it as well. Fold it over once, and secure it folded with the pin. Drop it into the jar. Repeat the following:

> Sealed with a pin
>
> In my jar, you stay in

Keep saying the words while you put a few drops of vinegar in the jar, and then a sprinkle of salt. Seal the lid tightly, and put the jar in a dark place.

The Witch Bottle

This type of charm is an old one, and is a classic spell to protect your home. It was originally intended as a way to protect against witchcraft, but its a common form of protection magick today. You will need a number of things, though you can adapt or modify the exact contents:

- A jar with a tight lid
- Pieces of broken glass
- Nails or pins (rusty is best)
- A pinch or two of dried rosemary and/or rue
- Vinegar

The exact amount of any items will depend a lot on how big a jar you use. Fill the jar with broken glass, rusty nails or other sharp bits of metal. Pieces of broken plates would work ok too. Fill the rest of the jar with vinegar, lemon juice or sour wine. If you want to be really authentic, add a little urine in their too.

Seal the jar tightly, and bury it outside your front door. A witch bottle will protect your house for years.

Protect Your Home

Seal your home up from any unwelcome or negative influences. I love this magic protection spell, and its also on the easy spells page because of its simplicity. You just need:

- A small handful of coarse salt

- A teaspoon or so of garlic powder or minced garlic

Stir the salt and garlic together, and put a few pinches of it on every windowsill and doorway into your house. If you can get every opening, that would be ideal. A bit on the fireplace hearth or the garage door, for example. Both salt and garlic are potent protective magick.

Herbal Protection

This spell is intended to add extra protection to you personally, not your home like the two spells above. The exact amounts of the herbs are up to you. You need:

- Rosemary
- Rue
- Lavender
- Basil (fresh if possible)
- Mint
- A handful of coarse salt

Run a hot bath, and toss in all your herbs and the salt. Let the bath steep for a few minutes before getting in. Sit and soak for a while, visualizing that your body is picking up protective energy from all the herbs in the water.

When you're done, save a bit of the water and herbs in a bowl and toss it outside.

Deflect Harm

Most reverse spells use mirrors to send the energy of the curse back to the person who sent it to you in the first place. You just need:

- 2 small mirrors, ideally on stands
- 1 black candle
- Sandalwood incense

Light the incense and let the smoke build up a bit around your altar area. Carve a deep X into the candle. You now have to set up your two mirrors so they face each other, and place the candle between them. It should look like repeating candles reflected deep within the mirror.

Light the candle, and let your eyes focus back and forth between the mirrors while you concentrate on the negative magick you are trying to reverse. Repeat the words:

> The magick upon me
> Be trapped this night
> Between these mirrors
> Never see light

Repeat the chant over and over, and visualize the curse becoming entangled in the reflections and sent back to the sender. Let the candle burn down on its own, but leave the mirrors facing each other for 1 month.

This spell should be done right at midnight for the most power.

Reversing Vinegar

This spell is a bit aromatic, so its best done in the evening when you're not going to be going out again immediately after. You need:

- Pure white vinegar
- Several pinches of fennel seed
- A small white bowl
- A piece of jet or onyx

The day before you plan on doing this spell, pour an ounce or two of vinegar into the bowl and add some fennel seed. Let this sit and "steep" until the next day.

On the next night, dip your fingers in the vinegar and dab a little bit on each wrist, your throat and your forehead. Just a little on the forehead because you don't want vinegar dripping in your eyes.

Sit with your eyes closed, and visualize white energy pushing out from your body at this points and forcing the negative magick back towards the sender. Force it away from you. When you are done, place the stone in the bowl, and leave it for 5 days. After that, pour the vinegar away into the ground.

Psychic Shield

This little charm bag is a potent Wiccan protection spell that you should keep on you at all times to protect against psychic attacks or other such phenomenon.

4 black candles

A small fabric bag in either purple or black

About a tablespoons worth of:

Agrimony

Anise

Horehound

Sandalwood

Rue

One piece each of:

Onyx

Jet

Hematite

Before you use it, you need to assemble and charge up this protection charm. Set the four candles up in holders in the shape of a square. In the middle, pile all the parts of your charm bag. Light the candles and concentrate on their light. Visualize it flowing into the center and filling up the herbs and stones you have there. Repeat the following:

By the light of four,

Harm me no more.

Repeat several times while you charge up the materials. When your satisfied, gather everything together and fill the bag with stones and herbs. Tie it tightly shut and place back in the center of the candles. Do the same visualization and repeat the same words again. When you feel that the bag is ready to go, snuff out the candles and start to carry the charm with you.

Remember that this Wiccan protection spell is intended to block psychic or astral energy, but it will do as a more general protection amulet in a pinch.

Unbreakable Shell Spell

This spell will create a protective "shield" around an object, protecting it from intrusion or theft. You'd use this with small items, like altar tools, jewelry or books. I wouldn't suggest it for your car.

- The item you want to protect
- 5 pieces of obsidian or jet
- Several feet of black yarn or string
- Ground rosemary

This spell makes use of the power of the pentacle, a typical Wiccan symbol. Set your item on a table or altar, and place the 5 pieces of stone in a pentagram shape around the object. Start to picture a shell being formed over your item.

Use the piece of string to lay out a pentacle, using the stones at the points of the star. Each line adds more energy to your growing shield. When the star is done, say out loud:

By the line unbroken,

Protect this token.

Use your finger to trace the pentacle in the air, above the one you made in stone and string. Repeat the words again.

Leave the item in its place overnight, and it should be protected from theft or harm.

Block & Lock

Set up an strong protection shield around yourself with a locked box and a little magick.

- A box you can lock
- 4 pieces of black glass
- Pen and paper
- Sprig of pine needles

The box can be just about anything, but it needs to be built in such a way that you can put a small lock on it. An actual lock-box would work, as would a jewelry box or any box with a hasp. The lock can be keyed or a combination. And for the glass, you can use beads or marbles as long as they are made from real glass.

Write your name on the paper, and fold it over. The spell is intended for your own personal protection, but you can use another person's name or several names of your own family.

Put the paper in the box along with the pieces of glass and pine needles. Lock the box and store is somewhere safe. If you used a lock with a key, keep the keep somewhere secure as well. This little protection box charm will help protect you from negative energy and any general problems in life.

Bouncing Back

This is another mirror spell that you can use to reflect difficulties away from you.

- A wall-mounted mirror
- A black crayon or marker

Choose a mirror you see or use often, not one that is tucked in a spare bedroom closet. The bathroom or your bedroom works best. Draw a pentacle in the top left corner, at least as large as your hand. Press your thumb to the glass at each point of the star, leaving five fingerprints around the pentacle.

Every day when you use the mirror, touch the center of the star to refresh the spell and bounce away any evil intentions in your life.

Wash Away a Curse

This spell is also listed elsewhere on the site, but its perfectly suited for this page too. It's a bit more elaborate than some other spells. You will need:

- 12 white candles

- 1 black or dark purple candle

- 1 cup of coarse salt

- 1 tbs lavender blossoms

- 1 tbs white sage (not green)

- 1 tbs chamomile

You can be liberal with the herbs, as long as they are in roughly the same proportions.

Perform this spell on the night after a full moon for the best results. On your altar (or right in the bathroom) make a circle with the 12 white candles. Put the black one in the middle. Don't light them just yet.

Run a hot bath, and add the salt and the herbs. Now light the candles and get in the bath. Get comfortable and repeat the following:

> By the light of moon's wane
>
> Cleanse my soul of this stain
>
> Let the spell be reverse
>
> Lift away this dark curse
>
> As I enter sacred space
>
> Return my soul to grace

Pour some of the bathwater over your head (keep your eyes closed!). Do this 3 times, and say the rest of the words each time:

I forgive what was done

Let the spell be undone

Stay in the bath until the water begins to cool off. When you get out, snuff out the candles but leave them in their circle. For the next 3 nights, relight them all and repeat the second part of the chant. After the 3rd night, relight the black candle and let it burn all the way out (if it's not already finished).

Candle Pentagram

You'll need to set this breaking spell out on a table or altar space that won't be disturbed for the duration of the spell. Your supplies are:

- Salt (fine, not coarse)
- 5 white candles
- Rosemary (oil or herbs)

On your table, sprinkle a fine line of salt to draw a pentacle. It doesn't have to be perfect but try to get it somewhat symmetrical. At each point of the star, add a few drops of rosemary oil or a sprinkle of dry rosemary (yes, right on the table top). Then set 1 white candle at each point.

Light each candle, starting with the one at the top. After each one, say the words:

>By the dark and the light
>
>Your spell ends tonight

Let the candles burn for one hour, then snuff them out. Do the same thing the next time, except let them burn all the way out.

Leave the candle stubs in place for another 5 days, so the entire spell is in place for a week. After that, any negative magick against you will be gone.

Additionally, I have a new page on how to break a spell that has more spells you can try against any negative magick.

Stay Away!

This is one of the most basic binding spells, best used to keep someone away who is bothering you. Be it an annoying co-worker or a pesty ex. It doesn't really stop any specific action, just keeps them out of your path. Your spell supplies:

- A piece of cardboard
- A long piece of black yarn
- Black marker

Cut out the rough shape of a person from the cardboard, and write the person's name on it in big letters with the marker. If you don't know their name, this spell won't be as effective but you can still give it a shot. Write how you know them instead (like "weird guy on bus").

Start chanting the following words, while you wrap the cardboard around and around with black yarn.

I bind you left,

I bind you right,

I bind you now,

Stay out of my sight

I bind you day,

I bind you night,

I bind you now,

With all my might

Keep repeating the words and wrapping until the little cardboard person is well covered-up. Tie three knots to secure the yarn.

You can then bury the charm outside, or just prop it up on your altar. If you do that, then repeat the chant each day to keep it working.

Black Candle Binding

Another traditional binding spell that involves knots and wrapping with string. Black candles can be hard to find, so you can use a dark purple, blue or brown one instead. You need:

- A black candle
- A length of rough twine
- A length of black yarn
- A length of black thread
- Sandalwood oil

The exact lengths of the cords doesn't matter, just use the same for all three. About 18 inches works well. Anoint the candle with sandalwood oil while you concentrate on the person you want to get out of your life. Wrap the black thread around the candle until you use the whole length, then tie it tightly. Then the yarn, and then the twine on top of that.

Light the candle, and let it burn out completely. Try to do this spell in the evening, letting the candle burn down overnight. Keep it somewhere safe and flameproof because the strings might catch fire as the candle burns down.

Shattered Glass Charm

This little charm bag is carried around with you to help protect you from the effects of the negative spell. After 7 days, the spell should be broken completely. Get your stuff together:

- A small black bag of a sturdy fabric
- Shards of broken glass (not more than 3)
- A piece of onyx, obsidian and/or jet
- A piece of copper wire, around 3 inches long

Twist up the bit of wire into a knot and drop it into the bag, saying "You are broken and have no power over me". Repeat the same words as you drop each piece of glass and stone into the bag. Tie the bag shut, also repeating the same words.

Now you need to have this bag with you for 7 days, including near your bed when you are sleeping.

Witch Bottle

This type of charm is an old one, and is a classic spell to protect your home. It was originally intended as a way to protect against witchcraft, but its a common form of protection magick today.You will need a number of things, though you can adapt or modify the exact contents:

- A jar with a tight lid
- Pieces of broken glass
- Nails or pins (rusty is best)
- A pinch or two of dried rosemary and/or rue
- Vinegar

The exact amount of any items will depend a lot on how big a jar you use. Fill the jar with broken glass, rusty nails or other sharp bits of metal. Pieces of broken plates would work ok too. Fill the rest of the jar with vinegar, lemon juice or sour wine. If you want to be really authentic, add a little urine in their too.

Seal the jar tightly, and bury it outside your front door. A witch bottle will protect your house for years.

• • • • • • • • • •

Healing Spells

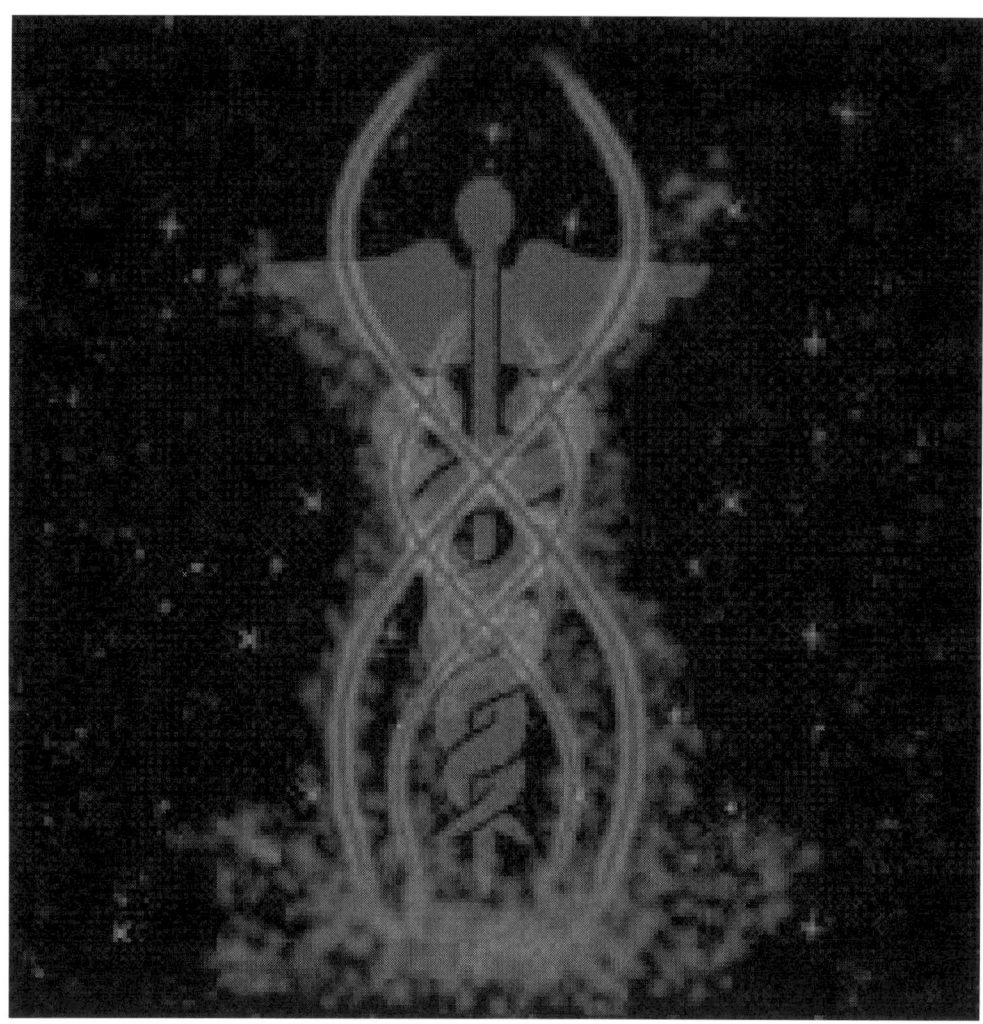

Power of 3

This spells uses the strength of the number 3 to help speed healing of an illness. It's best used when someone is ill, rather than injured. You can use this spell for yourself (if you are well enough to really focus on it) or for someone else. Your spell supplies are:

3 candles (1 each of purple, blue and white)

Myrrh oil

Mint oil

Sandalwood oil

3 pieces of quartz

3 small pieces of paper

Anoint each of the candles with all 3 oils, and set them up in an even triangle shape on your altar. Anoint the stones as well, and place one in front of each candle. Write the name of the ill person on each piece of paper, and place them in the center of the triangle.

Light each candle and focus on the person who is sick. Think about them being healthy and free of their symptoms. Picture them strongly in your mind as the candles burn. Repeat the following three times:

Magick mend and candle burn,

Illness leave and health return

Leave the candles to burn for 3 hours, then snuff them out. Your subject should soon start to improve, but you can add some extra power to your spell if you do the entire ritual for 3 nights in a row rather than just once.

Abracadabra Healing Charm

This is a very simple spell, but it's been around for thousands of years and comes from old occult practices. I thought I'd include it.

Write the word "Abracadabra" on a small piece of paper, and on each line, right the word with one less letter, like this:

ABRACADABRA

ABRACADABR

ABRACADAB

ABRACADA

ABRACAD

ABRACA

ABRAC

ABRA

ABR

AB

A

Roll the paper up and wear it around your neck. The belief is that the illness will disappear just like the word did.

Well-Being Spells

Craving Crystal

Use a crystal charm to help remind you of your weight loss needs, for a magickal prompt when cravings hit. All you need is:

- A piece of clear quartz

- A green candle

- A green bag or pouch (optional)

You'll have to do this weight loss spell during a waning moon, so anytime about 2 weeks after the full moon. Outside is best, but do the spell near a window if you have to be indoors.

Light your candle, and look up at the moon while holding the crystal. Repeat the following while you watch the moon:

> Goddess within
>
> Goddess without
>
> Guide me to my goal
>
> Easy my hunger
>
> Soothe my spirit
>
> Strengthen my resolve
>
> As I wish it, so mote it be

Concentrate on your goal of losing weight and eating healthier. Think about the foods you tend to crave, and how you need to be stronger around them. Send that energy into the crystal. Put out the candle when you are done, and carry the crystal with you. Use a green bag, or just tuck it in your pocket.

Now every time you are tempted to snack on something. take out the crystal and hold it in your hand. Ask yourself if you need this food, or are giving in to your craving. Draw energy from the stone to resist the food.

If you find it working well, you can recharge the stone by doing the same spell a month later. Ok, that's two. The page for free weight loss spells has a few more so you don't have to stop here. If your weight isn't the problem, you can try a more general beauty spell to jazz up your appearance.

Herbal Weight Loss Bath

All you need for this spell is a selection of herbal oils to add to your bathwater. You only need a few drops each of:

- Grapefruit oil
- Lemon oil
- Sage oil
- Basil oil

Run a deep bath for yourself, and add 4 to 5 drops of each oil into the water. Give it a swirl with your hands to mix, and get in. Have a nice soak, and enjoy the fragrance of the bath.

Then concentrate on the changes you want in your body, and rub the oiled water all over yourself. Visualize how you want to look (be realistic!) and feel your excess weight melt off into the water. Stay in the bath until the water cools.

If you can schedule this spell for a Saturday and/or during a waning moon, it will be even stronger. But as I say with many of my spells, magick can't produce miracles. Casting this spell, then sitting on the couch all day will give you no success. Eat better and exercise more, and this spell should give that edge to lose weight.

Chilled Binding

A symbolic binding (since you can't really tie your fridge closed) to help you improve your willpower and reduce snacking. Your supplies for this free weight loss spell are:

- A piece of black yarn, a few feet long
- Black candle

Light the black candle while you concentrate on improving your willpower and motivation to lose weight. Think about that while you tie knots in the yarn, about every 4 to 5 inches along the length.

Once it's knotted, take the yarn to your refrigerator and wrap it around the door handle several times and knot it tightly. While you do this, repeat the following:

> I bind you cravings, to stay away
>
> I bind you cravings, to stay away
>
> I bind you cravings, to stay away
>
> I am stronger than you today

Leave the candle somewhere safe to burn out. Then every time to go to the fridge, let the yarn remind you of your goal. If you find you tend to snack from the cupboard, you can cast this spell with a cupboard door instead

Changing Seeds

Nothing says change more than a sprouting seed that grows into a plant. So harness that transformation for yourself, as long as you have a little patience. This spell works best when you're trying to make some changes within yourself. You need:

- An egg
- A quick-growing seed (bean seeds work well)
- Potting soil
- A small piece of crystal
- A black marker

The first part is a little tricky, but you do need to get it right. You need a cup-shaped piece of egg shell to start your seed, so crack an egg carefully so that the top end comes off and you're left with about half an egg shell. Rinse it out gently and sit it out to dry for a few days before continuing.

Then use the marker to write a word on the outside of the shell to represent what you want to change. Place the little crystal in the shell. You'll want to use a type of crystal that relates to what you're trying to change (check the crystal chart) or use a plain piece of quartz. Fill the rest of the shell with soil. Press the seed into the soil and keep it moist. Use a cut piece of egg carton to hold the shell and leave it somewhere sunny.

Check the shell every day and take note in your mind as it starts to sprout and changes. Focus on that change and start to make your own changes as it grows. When it outgrows the shell, gently crack the bottom and then replant the whole thing into a larger pot so the plant can keep growing. Your own changes will thrive along with your plant

A Little Spark

When you're feeling sluggish or just generally "down in the dumps" try this energy spell to help rev you up a little. All you need is:

One orange candle

Orange yarn

- A cinnamon stick
- A heat-proof dish

Your length of yarn should be enough to go around the candle a few times. Wrap it around, and tie 3 knots in the yarn as you go so that they lie somewhat equally around the diameter of the candle. Set it in a candle holder and start to focus on your spell.

Concentrate on energy coming up from the Earth, and flowing up through your feet until it reaches your head. Once it's filled your body, light the candle. Say the following out lout:

Energy, power, rise up the tower,

Energy, power, rise up the tower,

Energy, power, rise up the tower

Holding one end of the cinnamon stick, put the other in the candle until it lights. Let it burn and smolder for a few moments, then set it in the fire-proof dish. Think about the heat of the flame until it burns itself out. Let the candle keep burning until it is done.

The Crystal Boost

This is a little charm bag you can carry with you to help bring a little extra strength and energy to your day. You need to have:

- A small cloth bag (white or blue)
- One each of:
- Bloodstone
- Citrine

Red jasper

Pyrite

A few chips of cedar wood

There is no real ritual to go along wth this charm bag. Just collect the stones you need, and put them in the bag with a few bits of cedar (or even just wood chips scented with cedar oil). Tie it closed and carry it with you to bring some energy along with you.

Gender-Empathy

If you're just looking into switching genders as a way of seeing how "the other half" thinks and feels, this is the spell you should try. It brings out the qualities of the other gender inside of yourself. This spell is the same regardless of your actual gender or orientation.

- 1 pink candle
- 1 light blue candle
- Length of pink ribbon
- Length of blue ribbon
- Knife
- Chalice
- Pure water

Wrap the blue ribbon around the pink candle, and then the pink ribbon around the blue candle. Set them up on either side of your altar. Light each one.

Focus your thoughts on the other gender and why you want to experience their viewpoint. Set the chalice filled with water in between the candles. This represents the female element. Gently heat the tip of the knife in the flame of both candles.

Hold the knife between both hands and dip the end of the blade into the water. This is the male. Keep holding the blade in the chalice and repeat the following:

Yang and yin

Which side is in?

Lady or man,

I know that I can.

Groom and bride,

See the other side.

Warlock and witch

Make me switch.

Wave the knife blade through each candle again and set it back down. Drink the water from the chalice. Let the candles both burn out on their own.

You should start to have shifted perceptions within 3 days. The spell will only last a few days once the effects get going. Use that time to really try to understand another gender's point of view.

Inner Understanding

This is a little different, but can help you gain some insight if you are struggling with your own gender identity. It can give you strength in dealing with it, and clarity when trying to make decisions.

- One white candle
- Cup of tea made with ginger, vanilla and allspice
- A piece of bloodstone

You can make the tea with a small chunk of whole peeled ginger root, steeped for 10 minutes in hot water. Then add a few drops of vanilla extract and a sprinkle of ground allspice. Should taste ok.

Light your candle, then set your teacup on the altar. Drop the bloodstone into the hot tea. Ask the Universe to help you understand your gender and what steps you need to take at this point in your life. Drink the cup of tea, preferably without swallowing the crystal.

Three Candles Joy

Add a little joy to your life when you need it the most. All you need is:

- 3 orange or yellow candles
- Cedar oil
- A few pinches of rosemary and marjoram

Rub oil on all three candles, and set them up on your altar. Light each one, then sprinkle each of the herbs on the table around the candles. Focus on the heat of the flames, and repeat outloud:

> Happiness and joy, come into my life
> Away with anger, stress and strife
> I am happy, I am free
> No more negativity

Hold your hands above the flames to feel their warmth. No need to scorch yourself. Be determined to see the positive side of things, and leave the candles to burn out.

Blooming Happiness

Bring positive fresh energy to your life with happiness spells and fresh flowers. You just need:

- Jasmine or Lilac oil
- One fresh flower, any kind
- Paper and pencil
- Yellow candle
- A heat-proof container

Light the candle, and write 3 things on the piece of paper that are making you unhappy right now. Put the paper in the candle flame and let it burn. You can drop it into the bowl when it gets going.

Rub a little oil on the flower, and breathe in the smell. Visualize your problems disappearing with the ash of the paper, and replace that stress with the joy of the flower. Set the flower in the bowl over the ashes, and leave on your altar to remind you to be happy.

Changing Winds

This is more of a spell to release anger and stress, but isn't that the first step to becoming more happy? Your supplies:

- A windy day
- A hill
- Basil
- Patchouli

Well, it's not mandatory that you have a hill for this, but you do need an open area outside for happiness spells like this. It does need to be windy.

Take your herbs to your chosen spot, and face away from the wind (so it's blowing on your back). Toss the herbs in the air and visualize your problems being blown away. Repeat the following:

> May the winds take my pain
>
> Make me happy once again

Then turn around and face the wind. Say:

> May the winds bring joy to me
>
> So that happy I will be

Stand in the wind for a few more moments, concentrating on the release of your problems and the acceptance of peace.

Beauty Within, Beauty Without

Already featured on the free witch spells page, this bath will help you feel more beautiful and shine that confidence. You will need:

- 1/2 cup raspberry leaves
- 1/2 cup marigold (calendula) petals
- Three yellow candles
- A teacup with flowers on it

Stir together the dried leaves and petals, then use half in a hot bath and half to make a small pot of tea. Strain the herbs out of your tea, and pour yourself a cup. Add a little honey if you want.

Light all three candles near your bathtub, and get in the bath. Soak while you drink your tea. Focus on the energy of the spell both inside of you, and surrounding you in the bath water. Repeat the following words:

> Beauty within
>
> Beauty without
>
> I am fabulous
>
> Without a doubt

Continue to soak in the bath until the water is noticeably cooled off. Before you leave the tub, you must finish the entire cup of tea.

You will be more confident in your looks, and others will see you as more attractive.

See Your Beautiful Self

Charge your reflection to show a more beautiful you. Your supplies for this beauty spell are:

- 1 glass of water
- A pinch or two of salt
- 2 pink candles
- Round, flat mirror

- Handful of rose petals (any color)

Set up a place to do your spell, preferably someplace that is usually quiet. Place your mirror flat on your altar or table, facing up, with a candle on either side. Add the salt to the water, and place the glass in the middle of the mirror. Light the candles and repeat the following:

> When I see me
>
> What do I see?
>
> When you see me
>
> What do you see?

Sprinkle the rose petals around the base of the glass, covering all the mirror surface. Visualize that people will start to see you differently, and that your image to others will be more beautiful, just like how your reflection is covered in rose petals.

Let the candles burn right down on their own, but make sure they aren't too close to the petals or something might catch fire. That's never good.

Loose Lips & Lies

This is a spell to help cause someone to come clean about any lies they are telling. The poppet will take a little time to put together but you don't have to make a work of art. A rough representation will do. Besides that, these are the rest of your materials for this spell:

- A cloth doll or poppet
- Stuffing for the poppet
- Dried thyme
- Dried rose petals

- One white candle

When you are making the poppet, you need to use stitches to "draw" the face (or at least the mouth). You can't draw the features on with a pen or marker. A few scraps of fabric and thread will work to make a doll. The person's name has to be on it, but that can be written if you don't want any more stitching to do. You can make the poppet up before you sit down to do the spell. Just make it in a human shape, stuffed with any stuffing but also with the dried herbs.

To do the spell, light the candle and have the poppet ready with a little pair of tweezers or scissors. Think about the person involved and the lies they have been telling. Say the following:

Through the mist of lies, deceit

The force of truth, you have to meet

Open lips and speak it true

Say what's honest, you must do.

Repeat the words twice, then slowly pick out the stitches of the poppet's mouth. When done, repeat the words another two times. Use tweezers to burn the bits of picked-out threads in the candle flame. This should should loosen up lips to let out the truth. Leave the poppet on your altar until you've gotten the honest information you want.

See Me Spell

This is a simple place to start, and it's a spell that doesn't change how you look but just makes people notice you. Great for social events where you are hoping to meet new people (for romance or otherwise), or even at work when you want your boss to see how you're doing.

- A small pocket mirror

A glass of white wine

A piece of clear quartz

A length of silver or white ribbon

This charm creates a strong positive energy that will attract people in your direction. Fill a glass with wine, and drop in the mirror. Let it sit overnight. Take it out the next day and let it dry (don't wipe it off though). After that, you're ready to go.

Set the quartz on the face of the mirror and wrap the ribbon around them both until it's secure. As you do this, repeat:

See me, see me, see me

In everything I do.

See me, see me, see me

Let this spell be true

Carry this with you, and people will start to pay more attention to you. The effects aren't permanent, and the charm will only last about 7 days.

Glim Glam

Like I said, most glamour spells are intended to make you more attractive so even though I have a page already for beauty spells, I'm adding another one here.

Silver glitter (yes really)

Rose oil

Primrose oil

Mix the two oils together in a little dish or saucer. Add a little silver glitter. Dip your index fingertip into the mix and draw a big heart on your stomach. Draw a circle inside the heart. There should be enough glitter in the oil that you can see the shapes.

Visualize positive and attractive energy coming from the image and covering your entire body. Leave the oil in place for the day (wear something comfortable over the image but not too delicate, the oil may stain). At the end of the day, take a bath to wash it away. The first day is the most powerful, but the effects can last up to 3 days after.

Lucky Orb

Not only will this spell bring you luck, it will make your home smell lovely. It uses the power of numerology and the lucky aspects of the 7.

- A small orange
- 7 fresh mint leaves
- 7 whole cloves

Concentrate on bringing new luck into your life, and use the pointed end of each clove to "pin" a mint leave into the skin of the orange. Like an old-fashioned Christmas pomander, except with mint.

Set the finished orange on the altar, and repeat the following lines:

May the universe smile down on me,

May the Gods bring me fortune.

May the winds bring me change,

May the spirits bring me luck.

Let the orange charm sit on your altar table overnight, and then it can hang somewhere in your home where you will smell its aroma. Your spell will be complete in 7 days, but you can let the charm hang longer if you want to. Just watch that it doesn't start to spoil or smell weird. Your luck will be tainted if you have rotten fruit hanging around.

Lucky Book

A free magic spell for luck designed for the literary lover.

- A slip of paper similar to a bookmark
- Your favorite book
- Red pen or marker

If you don't have a copy of your truly fav book, just choose one that you really like. It has to be a book you own, not a loaned library copy.

In big bold letters, write "Bring Me Luck" on one side of the piece of paper. Tuck it into the book on page 7, with about half of the paper sticking out. Then turn the top half of the bookmark down into page 11. Hold the book close to your heart, and ask the universe to bring you some unexpected good luck.

Place the book somewhere safe, preferably a book shelf surrounded by other books. Watch out for signs of new luck starting right away.

Wishing on a Star

The stars have great energy, and you can use that when making your wish spell. You'll have to do this on a clear night, preferably away from city lights if you can manage it.

- A piece of white paper
- The first star you see at night

Write your wish down on a piece of paper and fold it over once. Carry it with you outside to where you are going to watch for the star. Watch the sky and when you see the very first star, focus on its light for the rest of the spell.

Hold up the folded piece of paper so it blocks out the star, and repeat the following:

When you wish upon a star,

Your desires won't be very far.

Repeat 3 times. Lower the paper, and look at the star again. Repeat the words another 3 time while watching the light of the first star. Go back inside, and store the paper under your pillow. In a few nights, you'll see your wish start to come true.

• • • • • • • • • •

Candle Spells

Joyous Light

This is a household-type of spell that you use to reduce any tension that is becoming a problem and bringing in some happiness for the whole family (it works with roommates too).

4 candles, in all different colors

1 pink candle

A handful of fresh basil

Large piece of clear quartz

Sandalwood incense

You can do this spell on your altar but setting it up in a central place of the house is a better idea. Arrange the 5 candles in a circle. Set the crystal in the center, and then pile the basil leaves on top of it. Then light the candles.

Light the incense, and carry it through all the main rooms of the house. Take your time and let the smoke spread out. Once you've done that, return the incense to the place with the candles, and let everything continue to burn until out on their own. You should find that the tension and conflict should lift very soon.

New Beginnings Candle Spell

This is a good multi-purpose spell that can be used to give a bit of "oomph" to any new enterprise, whether it's a new job, relationship or just a new chapter in your life. It's an easy spell too.

- 2 white taper candles
- Rosemary oil

Anoint both candles with some oil, and set them in candle holders next to each other. Light one of them, and describe some of the "old" things you are hoping to get rid of. Focus on that for a few minutes, and then use the candle flame to light the second candle. Snuff out the first one.

Now list some of the new things that you are hoping to draw into your life at this new start. Be optimistic but realistic too. Leave the second candle burning until it is finished. You can reuse the first candle in another spell if you want.

Bless My Home Candle Spell

Let the bright warmth of your candles bring some added luck and happiness to your entire household.

    3 blue or purple candles

    3 sticks of incense in:

    sandalwood

    frankincense

    rosemary

    3 copper pennies

    A bell

The candles need to be large enough that a penny will fit in the candle holder under them. Set the candles up in a even triangle, and put one penny in each candle holder, under the candle.

Light one candle and say "Bring me hope", then light the sandalwood incense. Ring the bell.

Light the next candle and say "Bring me peace", then light the frankincense incense. Ring the bell.

Light the last candle and say "Bring me good fortune", and light the rosemary incense. Ring the bell one last time.

Set the incense burners within the candle triangle and let everything burn for at least an hour. An afternoon is better to really get the energy of the incense flowing in the house, but it isn't necessary. Snuff out the candles when you are done.

Dream Seeing

Use a candle to help awaken your inner psychic to bring intuitive dreams when you are sleeping.

- 1 white candle
- A Small square of purple and/or silver fabric
- 1 Black marker
- A Large piece of amethyst

Use the marker to draw an eye on the candle, the fabric and also on the stone. Set everything on your altar and light the candle.

Set the stone on the fabric so the eye's are touching. Visualize an eye in your own forehead that can open to see into your dreams. Hold the material to your forehead, with the eye drawing against your skin.

Watch the candle, and say "open sight" repeatedly while you watch the candle flame. Put the fabric back on the table, and then let the candle burn out on its own. Once finished, you can take the piece of fabric and sleep with it under your pillow for psychic dreams.

Financial Flame

You don't get too many candle spells for money, so I thought this would be a good spot for one. Your materials for this spell are:

- 2 candles, one gold and one green
- Patchouli incense
- Pine incense

Several acorns

Piece of paper

On the bottom of each candle, carve the rune Fehu (show on the right). Set them up in candle holders across from each other. Set the patchouli incense up next to the gold candle, and the pine beside the green one. Light everything and get the incense smoking.

Draw another Fehu on the piece of paper, and put your acorns on top. If you can't get acorns, smooth stones would work in their place. Both represent wealth and Earth energy in spells.

Let the candles both burn down until they are completely done, and leave the acorns or stones out on the altar until some extra money comes your way.

Burn the Negativety

When you have extra tension or negative energy in your life, this is the right Wiccan candle spell for you. It doesn't have to be bad energy in your home either. Whenever something is getting you down, do this ritual. You need to have:

1 black candle

Sandalwood oil

Dried mint, basil and/or white sage

Crush up your dried herbs so they are in really little pieces. Big flakes won't work very well in this spell. Rub oil all over your candle and get it nice and slick with sandalwood. Roll in your herbs so they stick all over the surface of the candle.

Set up the candle in a holder and light it. It might spark a little as the oil and herbs start to burn, so choose a location that is safe. As it burns repeat:

I banish negative energy,

I banish bad attitude,

I banish poor spirit

I welcome happiness and peace.

Say the words 3 times, then let the candle finish burning down. If there is any wax remaining, bury it out in the yard.

The Light of Happiness

This is a household-type of spell that you use to reduce any tension that is becoming a problem and bringing in some happiness for the whole family (it works with roommates too).

- 4 candles, in all different colors
- 1 pink candle
- A handful of fresh basil
- Large piece of clear quartz
- Sandalwood incense

You can do this spell on your altar but setting it up in a central place of the house is a better idea. Arrange the 5 candles in a circle. Set the crystal in the center, and then pile the basil leaves on top of it. Then light the candles.

Light the incense, and carry it through all the main rooms of the house. Take your time and let the smoke spread out. Once you've done that, return the incense to the place with the candles, and let everything continue to burn until out on their own. You should find that the tension and conflict should lift very soon.

Ignite The New Start Candle Spell

This is a good multi-purpose spell that can be used to give a bit of "oomph" to any new enterprise, whether it's a new job, relationship or just a new chapter in your life. It's an easy spell too.

    2 white taper candles

    Rosemary oil

Anoint both candles with some oil, and set them in candle holders next to each other. Light one of them, and describe some of the "old" things you are hoping to get rid of. Focus on that for a few minutes, and then use the candle flame to light the second candle. Snuff out the first one.

Now list some of the new things that you are hoping to draw into your life at this new start. Be optimistic but realistic too. Leave the second candle burning until it is finished. You can re-use the first candle in another spell if you want.

Red Triad Of Love

The number 3 really is powerful in the Wiccan world, which is why so many of my spells utilize it. This one is no exception. You'll need to have:

    3 slim red candles (the taper kind)

Length of red yarn or string

Rose oil

Yarrow oil

Lavender oil

Something sharp to inscribe the candles.

Carve a heart with a little pentacle inside on all three candles. It doesn't need to be artistically perfect, just a rough symbol is fine. Anoint each candle with one of the oils, and then bundle them together with the yarn so that their symbols are all touching the the middle of the group. Tie the string in a bow and set them up in a candle holder or dish.

Light all three candles and repeat the following:

Live, life, love

I ask for bessing from above

Three times three

Three times three

Bring them all to me

Let them burn down about a third of the way, and snuff them out. Then repeat again for the next 2 nights until the candles are done. You'll soon have a sign about someone new coming into your life for romance.

Fix the Rift

I thought I would add a different twist this time, with a candle love spell to repair a problem relationship. When you have a big fight or other type of split, try this spell to help mend things. It can't fix real fundamental differences between two people but it can help you both get over something that's happened.

- 1 thin lavender candle
- 1 white candle
- Powdered dry basil

This can be a little tricky to put together so be patient. Crack the lavender in half but don't cut the wick. So the wax is broken but the wick still runs through both pieces intact. While you work on this spell, focus on the rift you're trying to overcome and how you can improve things if you had another chance.

Rub some basil on the rough broken ends of the candle pieces and them fit them back together as closely as you can. Light the white candle and drip wax over the broken spot until you mend the lavender candle back into one piece.

Set up the lavender one, and light it. Leave it be until the flame gets to the point where the break is. At this point sit with the candle and focus on the flame as the candle passes through the joined spot, thinking about how you can make your relationship better. After it's passed the split, just let the rest burn out normally.

• • • • • • • • •

MONEY SPELLS

Pay a Bills

This spell is intended for use when you have a specific bill or debt to be paid, rather than just general prosperity. You need the following:

- Green Candle
- Patchouli or cinnamon oil
- Incense to match the oil
- A piece of paper

Use a pen or a pencil to draw a representation of the bill on the paper. Words and logos, along with the dollar figures. You will be burning the paper, so don't use the real bill. A photocopy may be more accurate, but will lack your personal energy so make your own drawing.

Anoint the candle with your chosen oil, and place the folded paper under the candleholder. Light the candle and the incense. Watch the flames and say:

> The candle burns
>
> It lights the way
>
> For money coming
>
> This bill will pay

Concentrate on this specific bill and why it's important to be paid off. Let the candle burn for about 15 minutes, then snuff it out. Every day, let the candle burn for another 15 minutes for a total of 7 days (make sure the candle is large enough). On the last day, remove the paper and light it in the flame to burn completely. Let the candle keep burning at this point until it goes out naturally.

Shimmering Silver

You'll need to perform this on the night of the full moon, and it must be a clear night so the light of the moon actually comes in through your window. Hopefully, that's not too inconvenient for you. All you need is:

- A cauldron
- 7 basil leaves, fresh
- Water, rain or spring
- 1 silver coin

If you don't have a cauldron, use a ceramic bowl, and the coin must have silver content at least.

Put the coin in the bottom of the cauldron, and pour water over it. Fill it at least half full, but it's up to you. Set the bowl in a window or on a table so that the moonlight shines on it.

One at a time, drop the basil leaves into the water, and say:

> By the light of the moon
>
> Send blessings soon
>
> Water and silver shine
>
> Wealth will be mine

Leave the cauldron or bowl until the next morning, then pour the water and basil out in the yard. Carry the coin in your pocket.

Abundance Spell

The energy of the flame will help draw new financial opportunities to you. Get your supplies together:

- A green candle
- Cinnamon oil
- Vanilla oil or extract
- A large denomination coin

Use something sharp to carve the word "Wealth" along the side of the candle and then anoint the word with cinnamon and vanilla. Put the coin in the bottom of your candle holder, set the candle in over top. Light the candle and let it burn down completely.

When the candle is done, leave the wax-covered coin in a safe place to help bring money into your life.

Harvest Husk Of Wealth

All you need to cast this spell is:

- One full leaf of dried corn husk
- A dollar bill
- A piece of green ribbon or yarn
- Patchouli oil

Flatten out the husk leaf and rub patchouli oil along the inside surface. As you work in the oil, repeat the following words:

With the power of the harvest corn,

Bring me money, from dusk till morn

Harvest the wealth

Bring Financial health

And let success be born.

Lay the dollar on the husk, and roll the two together into a tight tube. Tie it closed with the green ribbon, leaving a little extra ribbon for hanging. Hang it above a main door in your home and wealth will soon follow.

Money At My Door

5 pine twigs, roughly the same size

Silver and green ribbon

Patchouli oil

A dollar bill, preferably larger denomination (like a $20)

The twigs should be little branches, not pine needles. Gather your pine twigs and set them on your altar space, sitting on your money. Let them sit there for a week before you continue with the rest of this money spell.

Rub a little patchouli oil on each twig, repeating these lines each time:

Bring money through my door,

I need a little more and more,

Wrap up the twigs with the ribbon (yarn would work too), to make a little bundle. Leave some extra ribbon to make a loop so you can hang your money charm. Attach it to the main door in your house, either looping it over the doorknob or hanging by a nail. Doesn't matter which side, but it has to be on the main door of your home.

Leave the money charm hanging up until you have some extra money show up. Take it down after that. If you need more funds, make another charm but wait at least a week before doing the spell again.

Five Finger Cash-In

The number 5 is associated with abundance and wealth, so this Wiccan money spell focuses on that energy. The last spell did too, I suppose. Anyway, this is what you need for this spell:

- A green marker (washable)
- A silver coin

Do this spell on a Thursday if you can. Write the number 1 through 5 on the pads of your fingers, starting with 1 on the index finger to 4 on the pinky, then 5 on the thumb. Set the coin on a table or altar, and focus on why you need additional abundance in your life right now. If you don't actually need money, this spell may not be that successful.

Repeat the following, touching the numbered finger to the coin each time:

By the number 1, it's now begun,

By the number 2, let desires come true,

By the number 3, from debt be free,

By the number 4, I yearn for more,

By the number 5, it's time to thrive.

Then set your open palm over the coin, and repeat all 5 lines again. Leave the coin where it sits for 5 days, then carry it with you after that.

Wealth Welcoming Charm

Make your home more open to incoming prosperity with a welcome mat spell. Your spell supplies are:

- A door mat
- Sandalwood chips
- Dried basil leaves
- Patchouli herb
- A silver coin

Lift up the doormat, and sprinkle the sandalwood, basil and patchouli under it. Place the coin in the middle and replace the mat over top. Stand on the mat, face north and repeat:

> I welcome wealth into my home
>
> I sheppard it here, it will not roam
>
> From stress and worry I'm flying free
>
> Bring me new prosperity

Leave the mat and wait for new financial opportunities to come knocking.

Money Tea

You can make this into a ritual to have a freshly brewed cup of this tea every evening to help bring more money into your life. Or at least on Thursdays, the best day of the week for finances.

   1/2 tbs dried basil

   A pinch of dried dill weed

   Ground cinnamon

Brew up a cup of tea with the basil and dill, letting it steep for about 10 minutes. Strain out the leafy bits, and then add a light sprinkle of cinnamon. It's all very edible, but the flavor may not be that delightful. Add a spoon of honey if you wish.

These herbs all bring abundance energy into your body, and you should see some wealth after a few cups. Simple, but it's a money spell that works.

Bottles Of Cash

You will need a few items for this spell though:

- A small bottle with a lid
- 5 coins in different denominations
- 5 kernels of dried corn
- 5 sesame seeds
- 5 pieces of cinnamon stick
- 5 whole cloves
- 5 allspice seeds

- 5 peanuts

Choose a bottle large enough to fit everything but not too large. You want to fill the bottle. And the peanuts are just the edible parts and unsalted.

Put everything in the bottle and shake it up. While you're doing so, repeat the words of the spell:

> Riches be born
>
> Wealth be gained
>
> Poverty mourned
>
> Hard times tamed

Store the finished bottle near where you keep your wallet or purse, but you don't have to carry it with you (though you can if you want).

Bankroll Spell

Your spell supplies are just:

- A length of green yarn or ribbon
- A dollar bill (any denomination)
- Pine oil

Rub pine oil along the ribbon and start to tie knots. There are 5 knots, so try to keep them even along the ribbon length. Say each line along with one knot as you tie it:

Knot of one, the spell's begun

Knot of two, I make it true

Knot of three, prosperity

Knot of four, bring me more

Knot of five, the spell's alive

Roll the dollar bill up into a tube, and wrap the knotted ribbon around it. Wrap it tight enough to keep it from unwinding, but don't tie another knot in it. Leave the charm in your kitchen, somewhere safe.

Lucky Numbers

For the usual style of lottery, where you choose numbers on a ticket and wait to see what numbers are drawn to win, this is a spell to help get those elusive winning digits. You'll need:

- A pendulum
- A green candle
- Pine incense
- Sprigs of sweetgrass, lemon balm and borage
- Piece of paper
- Green marker

If you don't own a "real" pendulum, you can hang any small object from a length of chain or string. Draw a septagram (see image up to the right there) on the paper in green, and pile the herbs up in the center of the star. Light the candle and incense nearby.

Hold the pendulum by the end of the string so that the bob or object hangs in the center of the circle. Now comes the hard part. You need to think about getting that winning number.

First, focus on the first number. Start by saying "1" out loud and watching the pendulum. If it does nothing, say "2" and so on. At some point, it will give a shimmy and you should write that down as the first number. Then go on to the next digit until you have all the numbers you need for your specific lottery.

Get a ticket, and play these numbers for at least 3 weeks. It may not be effective for the immediate next draw.

Magic Scratch

This lottery spell is a little different, it's a spell you cast before you go to buy a scratch-type ticket. It should help guide you to pick a winning ticket.

- 3 acorns
- 5 dry corn kernels
- A small piece of malachite

Hold the acorns and corn kernels between your hands, as well as the piece of malachite. Rub your hands together, without letting any of the seeds drop out. Repeat the following:

With nuts and seeds

Where wealth leads,

Mix and match,

Choose and scratch

Now continue rubbing your hands together until all the pieces fall out from between your hands. The day after you do this spell, tuck the piece of malachite in your palm when you are pointing out the scratch ticket you want. Hopefully, you'll now pick out a winner.

• • • • • • • • •

Wicca Spells

Bad Habits Get Rid

Try to perform this spell on a Saturday night if you can. All you need is:

- A black candle
- Clove, sandalwood or cedar oil
- Something sharp to inscribe the candle
- A smooth piece of onyx or jet

Use your something-sharp (not your athame though), to write what your bad habit is on the candle. You don't have to be too descriptive, it's just a representation. Anoint the candle with the oil you are using. Light the candle and say the following:

Unwanted habits, please be gone

Leave me when the candle is done

Candle burn to remove all ill

By the power of want and the strength of will

Concentrate on your bad habit and how it makes you feel, see it burning away with the candle flame. Leave the candle to burn down until it is finished. Leave the stone by the candle while it burns. When the candle is burned away, carry the stone with you to remind you of your goal.

Banash A Curse Bath Spell

While the concept of "curses" has been thoroughly stereotyped by movies and books, they do exist. Just don't assume that every run of bad luck means that someone has cursed you.

- 12 white candles
- 1 black candle
- 1 cup of sea salt
- 1 tbs white sage
- 1 tbs lavender
- 1 tbs chamomile

The amounts don't have to be exact. You're not baking a cake here. Make sure you have white sage, not the green kind in your kitchen.

On the night after the full moon, make a circle of the 12 candles on your altar and place the black one in the center. Run yourself a hot bath, adding the salt and herbs. You can use a little cheesecloth bag for the herbs, if you don't want them floating loose in the water. Go light the candles, then sit by the tub and say the words of the spell:

> By the light of moon's wane
>
> Cleanse my soul of this stain
>
> Let the spell be reverse
>
> Lift away this dark curse
>
> As I enter sacred space
>
> Return my soul to grace

Get into the bath, and cup some water in your hands. Pour it over your head 3 times. Repeat the following each time:

> I forgive what was done
>
> Let the spell be undone

Then just relax in the tub until the water is cool. Snuff out the candles for the night. For the next couple of nights, relight all the candles and repeat the second part of the spell words. Let the candles burn for at least an hour, and then snuff out again. Do this until the black candle has burned all the way down. By then, you should feel the curse lifted from your life.

Piercing Love

Your supplies for this spell are:

- Small piece of red cloth
- Red candle
- Cinnamon oil

- 7 safety pins

Cut a heart out of the red cloth, at least 2 inches across. Bigger is fine too. On a Friday night, anoint the candle with cinnamon oil and light it. Say the following words as you fasten each of the pins to the heart:

Come forth my beloved,

And claim my heart

It's pierced seven times

Let loneliness depart

I bind it to yours

Forever and more

Now claim it and keep it

And lock the door

Leave the heart with the pins in front of the candle, and let it burn down completely. Afterwards, leave the pinned heart in a special place until love has arrived.

• • • • • • • • • •

That's All Folks!

Manufactured by Amazon.ca
Bolton, ON